BURKE'S

SPEECH ON CONCILIATION

WITH THE

AMERICAN COLONIES

EDITED BY

ERNEST R. CLARK

DEPARTMENT OF ENGLISH, EAST HIGH SCHOOL, ROCHESTER, N. Y.

NEW YORK ·:· CINCINNATI ·:· CHICAGO

AMERICAN BOOK COMPANY

British Constitution is established order
of government in Great Britain. Is
made up charters, laws, court decisions
customs,
Interpreted in the light of spirit + genius
of the English people.

INTRODUCTION.

EDMUND BURKE was born in Dublin, probably on January 12, 1729, though there is some dispute about this date. He passed his early school days in a town not far from his birthplace, under the tutorship of Abraham Shackleton, a Quaker schoolmaster of rare ability and moral worth, who had considerable influence in molding Burke's character. One characteristic which clung to him through life Burke manifested at an early age — when others were at play he was always at work. He entered Trinity College, Dublin, in 1743, and graduated in 1748. Much of his time at this period he spent in the libraries, gathering a store of useful information on many subjects which, later in life, proved to him a mine of intellectual wealth.

Burke's father was a solicitor, and Edmund prepared to follow in his footsteps; but, at the critical moment, his distaste for the law as a profession led him to abandon this career. He was, in fact, strongly attracted to literature, and he determined to adopt it as his calling. His father, indignant at this course, and angered at the overthrow of his most cherished plans, withdrew his allowance, and left his son to shift for himself in that most precarious of all callings. This was in 1755, and for the next year or so we hear little of Burke's doings. In 1756 he married Miss

Nugent, the daughter of his physician, and in his married life he must have been peculiarly fortunate, for he tells us himself that every care vanished the moment he entered under his own roof. Just about this time he published anonymously his first book, " A Vindication of Natural Society," — a clever imitation of one of Lord Bolingbroke's works against Christianity. Burke's design was to prove the absurdity of Bolingbroke's arguments by showing that they applied with equal force to civilization, and that, if carried out to their logical conclusion, we must deduce that society is an evil, and the savage state the only one in which virtue and happiness are possible. But so closely was the satire veiled, and so perfect was the imitation of Bolingbroke's style, that many of the best critics of the day firmly believed that the "Vindication" came from the pen of Bolingbroke himself, and that the arguments and conclusions were written in all seriousness. When we reflect that Bolingbroke at this time stood at the very summit of fame as a master of style, we perceive that Burke had attained no mean insight into the arts of literary composition. A few months later he published an essay on " The Sublime and the Beautiful," which was received with much applause. Perhaps the greatest good that resulted to Burke from these writings was the acquaintance with his brother authors to which they led, and the admission they gave him to the literary clubs of the day.

In 1759 Burke was engaged in collecting details of current events for a periodical called " The Annual Register." In this connection he became acquainted with men in public life, and among others with William Gerard Hamilton. In 1761 Hamilton went to Ireland as secretary to Lord Halifax, and Burke accompanied him. In 1763 Hamilton, who found Burke's services invaluable, procured him a pension of £300 from the Irish

Treasury. When Burke found, however, that in return for this benefit Hamilton expected him to bind himself body and soul to his service and to cast aside all loftier aims, he threw up the pension and severed his connection with this narrow-minded man. Not long thereafter, in 1765, Lord Rockingham was appointed prime minister, and Burke became his private secretary and, from that time on, his most loyal and devoted friend.

Now began Burke's political career, and that rare opportunity for good to his country and to the world at large of which he so well availed himself. We shall trace that career here in the briefest compass, for we are concerned now only with its outcome in his political writings.

He was returned in 1765 as a member of Parliament for the borough of Wendover, and in January, 1766, he made his opening speech, an argument favoring the petition sent to Parliament by the Stamp-Act Congress in America. " An Irishman, Mr. Burke, has sprung up in the House of Commons," said one of his contemporaries, " who has astonished everybody with the power of his eloquence and his comprehensive knowledge in all our exterior and internal politics and commercial interests." He represented Wendover until 1774, when he was returned from Bristol, a city at that time second in importance only to London itself. He sat in Parliament as the representative of Bristol until 1780, and thereafter for the town of Malton, which he continued to represent for the remainder of his parliamentary career. During this time his zeal for his country, and his love of virtue, justice, and good government showed themselves in a number of speeches which, by reason of their enduring literary qualities and the fire of eloquence which pervades them, are to-day regarded as classics.

These were troublous times in England as well as in America. It may be that the conflict for American independence was bound to arise sooner or later, that no conciliation or concession on the part of England could have repressed that deep longing for unrestrained freedom which was made manifest during the war for American independence; but the thing which above all others nourished the seed and fertilized the ground, and hastened the growth from a mere germ to its fullest development, was corrupt government in England.

No one saw this more clearly than Burke, and no one more courageously raised the warning cry. In 1770 he wrote his "Thoughts on the Cause of the Present Discontents," a masterpiece in which he attempted to paint in clearest colors the evils that had attacked Parliament by the growth of royal influence.

In 1774, 1775, and 1777 appeared his famous speeches on the American question — the "Speech on American Taxation," the "Speech on Conciliation with America," and the "Letter to the Sheriffs of Bristol." His keen foresight and indefatigable labors in search of truth enabled him to see the situation in its fullest light, and in all its bearings. Others there were who, through love of justice and humanity, favored a more generous policy on the part of England toward her colonies in America; but none among the English saw so plainly as did he the outcome toward which the English spirit was tending. Not for a moment did he shrink from his duty. He knew the members of Parliament with whom he was dealing, and he knew that arguments based on sentiment or abstract ideas of right would have no force. He spoke out in plain words, and appealed to their reason and their own interest. ("The question with me is not whether you have a right to render your people miserable, but whether it is not your interest to make them happy." Had his hearers been less corrupt, had they been but a little less blinded by their personal interests in respect to the public welfare, these speeches must have had their desired effect. Burke labored unceasingly to root out this corruption and to reform English politics. In his "Speech on Economic Reform," in 1780, he gives us a clear insight into the evils existing at that time in the relations between the Court and the House of Commons.

In return for all this disinterested service, and in recognition of his marvelous executive ability, we might well expect to see him filling one of the highest positions the government had to bestow. And yet he was never admitted into the Cabinet, nor did he ever hold any office above the rather subordinate one of paymaster — not even when his own friends and the party which owed everything to his efforts and ability came into power. There have been many attempts to explain this omission by his poverty, by his Irish birth and family connections, and by his sympathies with the Roman Catholics at a time when they were scarcely tolerated; but none of these causes seem adequate to account for such flagrant neglect, and, in truth, the matter has never been explained.

The Rockingham ministry had been dissolved in 1766, to be succeeded in turn by the ministries of Chatham and Grafton, and then by that of Lord North, who remained in power from 1770 to 1782, and who was largely responsible for the stringent measures against America. With the surrender of Cornwallis at Yorktown, Lord North's power came to an end, and Burke's friend, Lord Rockingham, once more became prime minister. He lived for only two months, and was succeeded in office by Lord Shelburne, who represented the Whig party and all the principles for which

Burke had so strenuously fought. To be sure, Shelburne was personally objectionable to Burke; but that does not excuse the latter from withdrawing his allegiance, and, least of all, for lending his support to Lord North — the man who, during his twelve years' previous ministry, had been responsible for many of the evils which Burke had done so much to reform. Lord North remained in power only eight months, and with him Burke withdrew from his office of paymaster, never to return.

He now devoted himself to a consideration of the English misrule in India — a question in which he had for some time manifested an active interest. The result of his study was given to the world in "The Nabob of Arcot's Debts," and the "Impeachment of Warren Hastings." The trial of Warren Hastings, Governor General of India, for crimes and misdemeanors, dragged on for six weary years, and in the end he was acquitted; but Burke's eloquent exposure and denunciation of the evils in India were not delivered in vain; for although the man he accused was not condemned, the system he opposed received its death-blow. "If I were to call for a reward," Burke said, "it would be for the services in which for fourteen years I showed the most industry and had the least success. I mean the affairs in India. They are those on which I value myself the most — most for the importance; most for the labor; most for the judgment; most for the constancy and perseverance in the pursuit."

We have now to consider the last period of Burke's life — that of the French Revolution. Burke was essentially conservative. "What he valued was the deep-seated order of systems that worked by the accepted uses, opinions, beliefs, prejudices of a community." He watched with an ever-growing distrust the rise of those forces in France which were to destroy this order, and in the "Reflections on the Revolution in France," which appeared in November, 1790, he gave voice to his feelings in almost frenzied tones. For the first time in his life he did not study thoroughly the subject he had in hand. He saw but one side of the question; he wished to see no other. The dangers of the new system blinded him to the disorders of the old, and he had nothing but scorn and invective to hurl against the revolutionists; not one word of sympathy for their wrongs or of excuse for their actions. The influence of this work was tremendous. "With a long resounding blast on his golden trumpet, Burke had unfurled a new flag, and half the nation hurried to rally to it — that half which had scouted his views on America, which had mocked his ideas on religious toleration, and which a moment before had hated and reviled him beyond all men living for his fierce tenacity in the impeachment of Warren Hastings."

Burke's attitude brought him much honor, but still more humiliation. The crowned heads of Europe applauded him, but his friends one by one dropped away. The climax came when he renounced the friendship of his lifelong companion, Charles Fox, because the latter could not follow him in his bitter denunciation of the French. This was in 1791. In August of the same year he wrote an "Appeal from the New to the Old Whigs," in which he tried to defend his views on the French Revolution, and to vindicate himself against the charge of having renounced his most avowed principles. From this time on he devoted himself to the French situation, and he went so far as to urge the English to interfere and wage war with France.

In 1794 Burke retired altogether from Parliament. The king and the Tories, well pleased at his attitude toward the French, were making arrangements to elevate him to the peerage when, in August, 1794, he was completely prostrated by the sudden death of his son Richard, to whom he was deeply attached.

The question of the peerage was dropped, but the king, in return for his long years of service, granted him a pension. As this pension had not been sanctioned by Parliament, the Duke of Bedford assailed it on the plea of corruption. In his " Letter to a Noble Lord," Burke repudiated this charge and showed how well he had earned this slight reward for long political services.

In 1795 he wrote his " Letters on a Regicide Peace," which, like all his writings of this period, are marked by his undying horror and hatred of the spirit of the French Revolution. After the death of his son he had little interest left in life, and he followed him to the grave on July 9, 1797.

And now we must consider what it was in Burke, that raised him from obscurity to a position whence he influenced the whole of Europe; what it was that ranked him among orators with Demosthenes and Cicero, among statesmen with Richelieu and Pitt, and among philosophical thinkers and eloquent writers with the greatest men of his time and of all time. The answer is ready at hand. To great breadth of intellect he added a strong will and a determination to gain a thorough knowledge of every subject within his range. He worked indefatigably, and his versatility was truly marvelous. It was difficult to find a subject in which he was not as much at home as though it had been his specialty. Add to these qualities a strong moral character, which led him to unwearied work in the cause of right and virtue, as he conceived it, and we have the elements of all true success.

He had no personal charms to recommend him; his gestures were awkward, his voice harsh, and his utterance displeasing.

We are even told that one of his listeners crept under a bench to escape a speech which, when published, he read till it was thumbed to rags. "I was not," Burke tells us himself, "swaddled and rocked and dandled into a legislator. I possessed not one of the qualities, nor cultivated one of the arts, that recommend men to the favor and protection of the great. I was not made for a minion or a tool. As little did I follow the trade of winning the hearts by imposing on the understandings of the people. At every step of my progress in life,—for in every step was I traversed and opposed,— and at every turnpike I met, I was obliged to show my passport, and again and again to prove my sole title to the honor of being useful to my country, by a proof that I was not wholly unacquainted with its laws and the whole system of its interests both abroad and at home; otherwise no rank, no toleration even, for me."

And so, inch by inch, he raised himself to the very pinnacle of fame. "No man of sense," said Dr. Johnson, "could meet Mr. Burke by accident under a gateway without being convinced that he was the first man in England."

The following characterization is taken from John Morley's excellent "Life of Burke": "Opinion is slowly, but without reaction, settling down to the verdict that Burke is one of the abiding names in our history, not because he either saved Europe or destroyed the Whig party; but because he added to the permanent considerations of wise political thought, and to the maxims of wise practice in great affairs, and because he imprints himself upon us with a magnificence and elevation of expression, that places him among the highest masters of literature, in one of its highest and most commanding senses. . . . . His passion appears hopelessly fatal to success in the pursuit of Truth, who does not usually reveal herself to followers thus inflamed. His ornate style appears fatal to the cautious and precise method of statement suitable to matter which is not known at all unless it is known distinctly. Yet the natural ardor which impelled Burke to clothe his judgments in glowing and exaggerated phrases, is one secret of his power over us, because it kindles in those who are capable of that generous infection a respondent interest and sympathy. But more than this, the reader is speedily conscious of the precedence in Burke of the facts of morality and conduct, of the many interwoven affinities of human affection and historical relation, over the unreal necessities of mere abstract logic. Burke's mind was full of the matter of great truths, copiously enriched from the fountain of generous and many-colored feeling. He thought about life as a whole, with all its infirmities and all its pomps. With none of the mental exclusiveness of the moralist by profession, he fills every page with solemn reference and meaning; with none of the mechanical bustle of the common politician, he is everywhere conscious of the mastery of laws, institutions, and government over the character and happiness of men. Besides thus diffusing a strong light over the awful tides of human circumstance, Burke has the sacred gift of inspiring men to use a grave diligence in caring for high things, and in making their lives at once rich and austere. Such a part in literature is indeed high. . . . . And we do not dissent when Macaulay, after reading Burke's works over again, exclaims, 'How admirable! The greatest man since Milton!'"

We, as Americans, owe to Edmund Burke a special debt of gratitude for his zeal and labors in our cause, and for the three speeches that should be placed on our shelves, side by side with those of our own great political writers.

To quote Mr. Morley once more: "Of all Burke's writings none are so fit to secure unqualified and unanimous admiration as the three pieces on this momentous struggle: the 'Speech on American Taxation' (April 19, 1774); the 'Speech on Conciliation with America' (March 22, 1775); and the 'Letter to the Sheriffs of Bristol' (1777). . . . . It is no exaggeration to say that they compose the most perfect manual in our literature, or in any literature, for one who approaches the study of public affairs, whether for knowledge or for practice. They are an example without fault of all the qualities which the critic, whether a theorist or an actor, of great political situations should strive by night and by day to possess. If the subject with which they deal were less near than it is to our interests and affections as free citizens, these three performances would still abound in the lessons of an incomparable political method. We should still have everything to learn from the author's treatment; the vigorous grasp of masses of compressed detail, the wide illumination from great principles of human experience, the strong and masculine feeling for the two great political ends of Justice and Freedom, the large and generous interpretation of expediency, the morality, the vision, the noble temper. If ever in the fullness of time,— and surely the fates of men and literature cannot have it otherwise,— Burke becomes one of the half-dozen names of established and universal currency in education and in common books, rising above the waywardness of literary caprice or intellectual fashions, as Shakespeare and Milton and Bacon rise above it, it will be the mastery, the elevation, the wisdom, of these far shining discourses in which the world will, in an especial degree, recognize the combination of sovereign gifts with beneficent uses."

Quotes from Bible & Shakespeare

CONCILIATION WITH THE AMERICAN COLONIES.[1]

I HOPE, Sir, that, notwithstanding the austerity of the Chair, your good nature will incline you to some degree of indulgence towards human frailty. You will not think it unnatural, that those who have an object depending, which strongly engages their hopes and fears, should be somewhat inclined to superstition. As I came into the House full of anxiety about the event of my motion, I found, to my infinite surprise, that the grand penal bill, by which we had passed sentence on the trade and sustenance of America, is to be returned to us from the other House.[2] I do confess, I could not help looking on this event as a fortunate omen. I look upon it as a sort of providential favor; by which we are put once more in possession of our deliberative capacity, upon a business so very questionable in its nature, so very uncertain in its issue. By the return of this bill, which seemed to have

[1] This speech was delivered by Edmund Burke in the House of Commons, March 22, 1775, on moving his resolutions for conciliation with the colonies.

[2] House of Lords. A few weeks previous, Lord North, at that time Prime Minister of England, had proposed an act to restrain the trade and commerce of the provinces of Massachusetts Bay and New Hampshire, the colonies of Connecticut and Rhode Island, and Providence Plantation, in North America, to Great Britain, Ireland, and the British Islands in the West Indies; and to prohibit such provinces and colonies from carrying on any fishery on the banks of Newfoundland, and other places therein mentioned, under certain conditions and limitations. Burke had spoken with great indignation against the injustice of this bill.

taken its flight forever, we are, at this very instant, nearly as free to choose a plan for our American government as we were on the first day of the session.   If, Sir, we incline to the side of concilia-tion, we are not at all embarrassed (unless we please to make ourselves so) by any incongruous mixture of coercion and re-straint.   We are therefore called upon, as it were by a superior warning voice, again to attend to America; to attend to the whole of it together; and to review the subject with an unusual degree of care and calmness.

Surely it is an awful subject; or there is none so on this side of the grave.   When I first had the honor of a seat in this House, the affairs of that continent pressed themselves upon us, as the most important and most delicate object of parliamentary atten-tion.   My little share in this great deliberation oppressed me.   I found myself a partaker in a very high trust; and having no sort of reason to rely on the strength of my natural abilities for the proper execution of that trust, I was obliged to take more than common pains to instruct myself in everything which relates to our colonies.   I was not less under the necessity of forming some fixed ideas concerning the general policy of the British empire.   Something of this sort seemed to be indispensable, in order, amidst so vast a fluctuation of passions and opinions, to concenter my thoughts, to ballast my conduct, to preserve me from being blown about by every wind of fashionable doctrine.   I really did not think it safe, or manly, to have fresh principles to seek upon every fresh mail which should arrive from America.

At that period[1] I had the fortune to find myself in perfect con-currence with a large majority in this House.   Bowing under that high authority, and penetrated with the sharpness and strength of that early impression, I have continued ever since, without the least deviation, in my original sentiments.   Whether this be owing to an obstinate perseverance in error, or to a religious adherence to what appears to me truth and reason, it is in your equity to judge.

Sir, Parliament having an enlarged view of objects, made, during

[1] The time of the repeal of the Stamp Act.

this interval, more frequent changes in their sentiments and their conduct, than could be justified in a particular person upon the contracted scale of private information.   But though I do not hazard anything approaching to censure on the motives of former Parliaments to all those alterations, one fact is undoubted — that under them the state of America has been kept in continual agitation.   Everything administered as remedy to the public complaint, if it did not produce, was at least followed by, an heightening of the distemper; until, by a variety of experiments, that important country has been brought into her present situation — a situation which I will not miscall, which I dare not name, which I scarcely know how to comprehend in the terms of any description.

In this posture, Sir, things stood at the beginning of the session. About that time, a worthy member[1] of great parliamentary experience, who, in the year 1766, filled the chair of the American Committee with much ability, took me aside; and, lamenting the present aspect of our politics, told me things were come to such a pass that our former methods of proceeding in the House would be no longer tolerated.   That the public tribunal (never too indulgent to a long and unsuccessful opposition) would now scrutinize our conduct with unusual severity.   That the very vicissitudes and shiftings of ministerial measures, instead of convicting their authors of inconstancy and want of system, would be taken as an occasion of charging us with a predetermined discontent which nothing could satisfy, whilst we accused every measure of vigor as cruel, and every proposal of lenity as weak and irresolute.   The public, he said, would not have patience to see us play the game out with our adversaries : we must produce our hand.   It would be expected that those, who for many years had been active in such affairs, should show that they had formed some clear and decided idea of the principles of colony government; and were capable of drawing out something like a platform of the ground, which might be laid for future and permanent tranquillity.

1 Mr. Rose Fuller.

I felt the truth of what my honorable friend represented; but I felt my situation too. His application might have been made with far greater propriety to many other gentlemen. No man was indeed ever better disposed, or worse qualified, for such an undertaking than myself. Though I gave so far into his opinion that I immediately threw my thoughts into a sort of parliamentary form, I was by no means equally ready to produce them. It generally argues some degree of natural impotence of mind, or some want of knowledge of the world, to hazard plans of government except from a seat of authority. Propositions are made, not only ineffectually, but somewhat disreputably, when the minds of men are not properly disposed for their reception; and for my part, I am not ambitious of ridicule, not absolutely a candidate for disgrace.

Besides, Sir, to speak the plain truth, I have in general no very exalted opinion of the virtue of paper government,[1] nor of any politics in which the plan is to be wholly separated from the execution. But when I saw that anger and violence prevailed every day more and more, and that things were hastening toward an incurable alienation of our colonies, I confess my caution gave way. I felt this as one of those few moments in which decorum yields to a higher duty. Public calamity is a mighty leveler; and there are occasions when any, even the slightest, chance of doing good must be laid hold on, even by the most inconsiderable person.

To restore order and repose to an empire so great and so distracted as ours, is, merely in the attempt, an undertaking that would ennoble the flights of the highest genius, and obtain pardon for the efforts of the meanest understanding. Struggling a good while with these thoughts, by degrees I felt myself more firm. I derived, at length, some confidence from what in other circumstances usually produces timidity. I grew less anxious, even from the idea of my own insignificance. For, judging of what you are by what you ought to be, I persuaded myself that you would not reject a reasonable proposition because it had nothing but its

1 "Paper government," i.e., measures proposed in a bill, but not yet carried out.

reason to recommend it. On the other hand, being totally destitute of all shadow of influence, natural or adventitious, I was very sure that, if my proposition were futile or dangerous, if it were weakly conceived, or improperly timed, there was nothing exterior to it of power to awe, dazzle, or delude you. You will see it just as it is; and you will treat it just as it deserves.

The proposition is peace. Not peace through the medium of war; not peace to be hunted through the labyrinth of intricate and endless negotiations; not peace to arise out of universal discord, fomented from principle, in all parts of the empire; not peace to depend on the juridical determination of perplexing questions, or the precise marking of the shadowy boundaries of a complex government. It is simple peace, sought in its natural course, and in its ordinary haunts. It is peace sought in the spirit of peace, and laid in principles purely pacific. I propose, by removing the ground of the difference, and by restoring the *former unsuspecting confidence of the colonies in the mother country*, to give permanent satisfaction to your people, and (far from a scheme of ruling by discord) to reconcile them to each other in the same act and by the bond of the very same interest which reconciles them to British government.

My idea is nothing more. Refined policy ever has been the parent of confusion; and ever will be so, as long as the world endures. Plain good intention, which is as easily discovered at the first view as fraud is surely detected at last, is, let me say, of no mean force in the government of mankind. Genuine simplicity of heart is a healing and cementing principle. My plan, therefore, being formed upon the most simple grounds imaginable, may disappoint some people when they hear it. It has nothing to recommend it to the pruriency[1] of curious ears. There is nothing at all new and captivating in it. It has nothing of the splendor of the project which has been lately laid upon your table by the noble lord in the blue ribbon.[2] It does not propose

---

[1] Eager desire.

[2] The blue ribbon was the badge of the Order of the Garter. The reference here is to Lord North, who had been made a knight of the Garter. He

to fill your lobby with squabbling colony agents, who will require the interposition of your mace,[1] at every instant, to keep the peace amongst them.   It does not institute a magnificent auction of finance, where captivated provinces come to general ransom by
5 bidding against each other, until you knock down the hammer, and determine a proportion of payments beyond all the powers of algebra to equalize and settle.

The plan which I shall presume to suggest, derives, however, one great advantage from the proposition and registry of that no-
10 ble lord's project.   The idea of conciliation is admissible.   First, the House, in accepting the resolution moved by the noble lord, has admitted, notwithstanding the menacing front of our address, notwithstanding our heavy bill of pains and penalties, that we do not think ourselves precluded from all ideas of free grace and
15 bounty.

The House has gone further; it has declared conciliation admissible, *previous* to any submission on the part of America.   It has even shot a good deal beyond that mark, and has admitted that the complaints of our former mode of exerting the right of
20 taxation were not wholly unfounded.   That right thus exerted is allowed to have had something reprehensible in it — something unwise, or something grievous; since, in the midst of our heat and resentment, we, of ourselves, have proposed a capital alteration, and, in order to get rid of what seemed so very exception-
25 able, have instituted a mode that is altogether new — one that is, indeed, wholly alien from all the ancient methods and forms of Parliament.

The *principle* of this proceeding is large enough for my purpose. The means proposed by the noble lord for carrying his ideas into
30 execution, I think, indeed, are very indifferently suited to the end; and this I shall endeavor to show you before I sit down.   But, for

had introduced a bill proposing that any province or colony which should make provision for their common defense should be exempt from taxation. This offer was rejected by the colonies.

1 The emblem of authority lying on the Speaker's table; hence, the sergeant-at-arms of the House.

the present, I take my ground on the admitted principle. I mean to give peace. Peace implies reconciliation; and, where there has been a material dispute, reconciliation does in a manner always imply concession on the one part or on the other. In this state of things, I make no difficulty in affirming that the proposal ought to originate from us. Great and acknowledged force is not impaired, either in effect or in opinion, by an unwillingness to exert itself. The superior power may offer peace with honor and with safety. Such an offer from such a power will be attributed to magnanimity. But the concessions of the weak are the concessions of fear. When such a one is disarmed, he is wholly at the mercy of his superior; and he loses forever that time and those chances, which, as they happen to all men, are the strength and resources of all inferior power.

The capital leading questions on which you must this day decide, are these two: first, whether you ought to concede; and secondly, what your concession ought to be. On the first of these questions we have gained (as I have just taken the liberty of observing to you) some ground. But I am sensible that a good deal more is still to be done. Indeed, Sir, to enable us to determine both on the one and the other of these great questions with a firm and precise judgment, I think it may be necessary to consider distinctly the true nature and the peculiar circumstances of the object which we have before us. Because, after all our struggle, whether we will or not, we must govern America according to that nature, and to those circumstances; and not according to our own imaginations; nor according to abstract ideas of right; by no means according to mere general theories of government, the resort to which appears to me, in our present situation, no better than arrant trifling. I shall therefore endeavor, with your leave, to lay before you some of the most material of these circumstances in as full and as clear a manner as I am able to state them.

The first thing that we have to consider with regard to the nature of the object is — the number of people in the colonies. I have taken for some years a good deal of pains on that point. I

can by no calculation justify myself in placing the number below
two millions of inhabitants of our own European blood and color;
besides at least 500,000 others, who form no inconsiderable part
of the strength and opulence of the whole. This, Sir, is, I believe,
5 about the true number. There is no occasion to exaggerate,
where plain truth is of so much weight and importance. But
whether I put the present numbers too high or too low is a matter of little moment. Such is the strength with which population shoots in that part of the world, that, state the numbers as
10 high as we will, whilst the dispute continues, the exaggeration
ends. Whilst we are discussing any given magnitude, they are
grown to it. Whilst we spend our time in deliberating on the
mode of governing two millions, we shall find we have millions
more to manage. Your children do not grow faster from infancy
15 to manhood, than they spread from families to communities, and
from villages to nations.

I put this consideration of the present and the growing numbers in the front of our deliberation; because, Sir, this consideration
will make it evident to a blunter discernment than yours, that no
20 partial, narrow, contracted, pinched, occasional system will be at
all suitable to such an object. It will show you that it is not to
be considered as one of those *minima*[1] which are out of the eye
and consideration of the law; not a paltry excrescence of the
state; not a mean dependent, who may be neglected with little
25 damage and provoked with little danger. It will prove that
some degree of care and caution is required in the handling such
an object; it will show that you ought not, in reason, to trifle with
so large a mass of the interests and feelings of the human race.
You could at no time do so without guilt; and be assured you will
30 not be able to do it long with impunity.

But the population of this country,— the great and growing population,— though a very important consideration, will lose much
of its weight if not combined with other circumstances. The commerce of your colonies is out of all proportion beyond the num-

[1] Plural of the Latin adjective *minimum*, meaning " of the smallest possible amount "; hence, matters of no consequence; trifles.

bers of the people. This ground of their commerce indeed has been trod some days ago, and with great ability, by a distinguished person,[1] at your bar. This gentleman, after thirty-five years, — it is so long since he first appeared at the same place to plead for the commerce of Great Britain, — has come again before you to plead the same cause, without any other effect of time, than that, to the fire of imagination and extent of erudition which even then marked him as one of the first literary characters of his age, he has added a consummate knowledge in the commercial interest of his country, formed by a long course of enlightened and discriminating experience.

Sir, I should be inexcusable in coming after such a person with any detail, if a great part of the members who now fill the House had not the misfortune to be absent when he appeared at your bar. Besides, Sir, I propose to take the matter at periods of time somewhat different from his. There is, if I mistake not, a point of view, from whence if you will look at this subject, it is impossible that it should not make an impression upon you.

I have in my hand two accounts: one a comparative state[2] of the export trade of England to its colonies, as it stood in the year 1704, and as it stood in the year 1772; the other a state of the export trade of this country to its colonies alone, as it stood in 1772, compared with the whole trade of England to all parts of the world (the colonies included) in the year 1704. They are from good vouchers; the latter period from the accounts on your table, the earlier from an original manuscript of Davenant, who first established the inspector-general's office, which has been ever since his time so abundant a source of parliamentary information.

The export trade to the colonies consists of three great branches. The African, which, terminating almost wholly in the colonies, must be put to the account of their commerce; the West Indian; and the North American. All these are so interwoven that the attempt to separate them would tear to pieces the

[1] A Mr. Glover, who had appeared before the House in a plea for peace with the colonies.

[2] Statement.

contexture of the whole, and if not entirely destroy, would very much depreciate the value of all the parts. I therefore consider these three denominations to be, what in effect they are, one trade.

The trade to the colonies, taken on the export side, at the beginning of this century, that is, in the year 1704, stood thus:

Exports to North America and the West Indies..	£483,265
To Africa....................................	86,665
	£569,930

In the year 1772, which I take as a middle year between the highest and lowest of those lately laid on your table, the account was as follows:

To North America and the West Indies.........£4,791,734
To Africa....................................	866,398
To which if you add the export trade from Scot- land, which had in 1704 no existence........	364,000
	£6,022,132

From five hundred and odd thousand, it has grown to six millions. It has increased no less than twelve-fold. This is the state of the colony trade, as compared with itself at these two periods within this century; and (this is a matter for meditation.) But this is not all. Examine my second account. See how the export trade to the colonies alone in 1772 stood in the other point of view, that is, as compared to the whole trade of England in 1704.

The whole export trade of England, including that to the colonies, in 1704.................	£6,509,000
Export to the colonies alone, in 1772..........	6,024,000
Difference £	485,000

The trade with America alone is now within less than £500,000 of being equal to what this great commercial nation, England, carried on at the beginning of this century with the whole world! If I had taken the largest year of those on your table, it would rather have exceeded. But, it will be said, is not this American trade an unnatural protuberance, that has drawn the juices from the rest of the body? The reverse. It is the very food that has nourished every other part into its present magnitude. Our general trade has been greatly augmented, and augmented more or less in almost every part to which it ever extended; but with this material difference, that of the six millions which in the beginning of the century constituted the whole mass of our export commerce, the colony trade was but one-twelfth part; it is now (as a part of sixteen millions) considerably more than a third of the whole. This is the relative proportion of the importance of the colonies at these two periods; and all reasoning concerning our mode of treating them must have this proportion as its basis, or it is a reasoning weak, rotten, and sophistical.

Mr. Speaker, I cannot prevail on myself to hurry over this great consideration. It is good for us to be here. We stand where we have an immense view of what is, and what is past. Clouds, indeed, and darkness rest upon the future. Let us, however, before we descend from this noble eminence, reflect that this growth of our national prosperity has happened within the short period of the life of man. It has happened within sixty-eight years. There are those alive whose memory might touch the two extremities. For instance, my Lord Bathurst might remember all the stages of the progress. He was in 1704 of an age at least to be made to comprehend such things. He was then old enough *acta parentum jam legere, et quæ sit poterit cognoscere virtus.*[1] Suppose, Sir, that the angel of this auspicious youth, foreseeing the many virtues which made him one of the most amiable, as he is one of the most fortunate, men of his age, had opened to him in vision, that when, in the fourth generation, the third prince[2] of the House of Brunswick had sat twelve years on the throne of that nation, which (by the happy issue of moderate and healing coun-

---

[1] "To read the achievements of his fathers, and be able to understand what virtue is" See Vergil, Eclogue iv.

[2] The reference here is to George III, who was King of England at the time of the delivery of this speech.

cils) was to be made Great Britain,[1] he should see his son, Lord
Chancellor of England, turn back the current of hereditary
dignity to its fountain, and raise him to a higher rank of peerage,
whilst he enriched the family with a new one.   If amidst these
5 bright and happy scenes of domestic honor and prosperity, that
angel should have drawn up the curtain, and unfolded the rising
glories of his country, and whilst he was gazing with admiration
on the then commercial grandeur of England, the genius should
point out to him a little speck, scarce visible in the mass of the
10 national interest, a small seminal principle,[2] rather than a formed
body, and should tell him: "Young man, there is America,
which at this day serves for little more than to amuse you with
stories of savage men and uncouth manners, yet shall, before you
taste of death, show itself equal to the whole of that commerce
15 which now attracts the envy of the world.   Whatever England
has been growing to by a progressive increase of improvement,
brought in by varieties of people, by succession of civilizing conquests and civilizing settlements in a series of seventeen hundred
years, you shall see as much added to her by America in the
20 course of a single life!"—if this state of his country had been
foretold to him, would it not require all the sanguine credulity of
youth, and all the fervid glow of enthusiasm, to make him believe
it?   Fortunate man, he has lived to see it!   Fortunate indeed, if
he lives to see nothing that shall vary the prospect, and cloud the
25 setting of his day!

Excuse me, Sir, if, turning from such thoughts, I resume this
comparative view once more.   You have seen it on a large scale;
look at it on a small one.   I will point out to your attention a
particular instance of it in the single province of Pennsylvania.
30 In the year 1704, that province called for £11,459 in value of
your commodities, native and foreign.   This was the whole.
What did it demand in 1772?   Why, nearly fifty times as much;
for in that year the export to Pennsylvania was £507,909, nearly

---

1 The name of Great Britain was not formally used to indicate the kingdom
until after the union of the Scottish and English Parliaments in 1707.
2 "Seminal principle," i.e., germ.

equal to the export to all the colonies together in the first period.

I choose, Sir, to enter into these minute and particular details; because generalities, which in all other cases are apt to heighten and raise the subject, have here a tendency to sink it.   When we speak of the commerce with our colonies, fiction lags after truth, invention is unfruitful, and imagination cold and barren.

So far, Sir, as to the importance of the object in view of its commerce, as concerned in the exports from England.   If I were to detail the imports, I could show how many enjoyments they procure which deceive the burthen[1] of life; how many materials which invigorate the springs of national industry, and extend and animate every part of our foreign and domestic commerce.   This would be a curious subject indeed — but I must prescribe bounds to myself in a matter so vast and various.

I pass, therefore, to the colonies in another point of view — their agriculture.   This they have prosecuted with such a spirit, that, besides feeding plentifully their own growing multitude, their annual export of grain, comprehending rice, has some years ago exceeded a million in value.   Of their last harvest, I am persuaded they will export much more.   At the beginning of the century some of these colonies imported corn from their mother country.

For some time past, the Old World has been fed from the New. The scarcity which you have felt would have been a desolating famine, if this child of your old age, with a true filial piety, with a Roman charity, had not put the full breast of its youthful exuberance to the mouth of its exhausted parent.[2]

As to the wealth which the colonies have drawn from the sea by their fisheries, you had all that matter fully opened at your bar.   You surely thought these acquisitions of value, for they seemed even to excite your envy; and yet the spirit by which that enterprising employment has been exercised, ought rather, in

1 Old form of "burden."

2 An allusion to the story of a Roman girl who, when her father was imprisoned and left to starve, obtained entrance to his cell, and nourished him from her own breast.

my opinion, to have raised your esteem and admiration. And pray, Sir, what in the world is equal to it? Pass by the other parts, and look at the manner in which the people of New England have of late carried on the whale fishery. Whilst we follow them among the tumbling mountains of ice, and behold them penetrating into the deepest frozen recesses of Hudson Bay and Davis Straits, whilst we are looking for them beneath the arctic circle, we hear that they have pierced into the opposite region of polar cold, that they are at the antipodes, and engaged under the frozen serpent[1] of the south. Falkland Island,[2] which seemed too remote and romantic an object for the grasp of national ambition, is but a stage and resting place in the progress of their victorious industry. Nor is the equinoctial heat more discouraging to them than the accumulated winter of both the poles. We know that whilst some of them draw the line and strike the harpoon on the coast of Africa, others run the longitude, and pursue their gigantic game along the coast of Brazil. No sea but what is vexed by their fisheries! No climate that is not witness to their toils! Neither the perseverance of Holland, nor the activity of France, nor the dexterous and firm sagacity of English enterprise, ever carried this most perilous mode of hard industry to the extent to which it has been pushed by this recent people—a people who are still, as it were, but in the gristle, and not yet hardened into the bone of manhood. When I contemplate these things; when I know that the colonies in general owe little or nothing to any care of ours, and that they are not squeezed into this happy form by the constraints of watchful and suspicious government—but that, through a wise and salutary neglect, a generous nature has been suffered to take her own way to perfection: when I reflect upon these effects, when I see how profitable they have been to us, I feel all the pride of power sink, and all presumption in the wisdom of human contrivances melt and die away within me. My rigor relents. I pardon something to the spirit of liberty.

[1] A constellation seen within the antarctic circle.
[2] The largest of a group of islands off the southeast coast of South America, belonging to Great Britain.

I am sensible, Sir, that all which I have asserted in my detail, is admitted in the gross; but that quite a different conclusion is drawn from it. America, gentlemen say, is a noble object. It is an object well worth fighting for. Certainly it is, if fighting a people be the best way of gaining them. Gentlemen in this re- spect will be led to their choice of means by their complexions and their habits. Those who understand the military art will, of course, have some predilection for it. Those who wield the thunder of the state, may have more confidence in the efficacy of arms. But I confess, possibly for want of this knowledge, my opinion is much more in favor of prudent management, than of force; considering force not as an odious, but a feeble, instru- ment, for preserving a people so numerous, so active, so growing, so spirited as this, in a profitable and subordinate connection with us.

First, Sir, permit me to observe, that the use of force alone is but *temporary.* It may subdue for a moment; but it does not remove the necessity of subduing again: and a nation is not governed, which is perpetually to be conquered.

My next objection is its *uncertainty.* Terror is not always the effect of force; and an armament is not a victory. If you do not succeed, you are without resource; for, conciliation failing, force remains; but, force failing, no further hope of reconciliation is left. Power and authority are sometimes bought by kindness; but they can never be begged as alms by an impoverished and defeated violence.

A further objection to force is, that you *impair the object* by your very endeavors to preserve it. The thing you fought for is not the thing which you recover — but depreciated, sunk, wasted, and consumed in the contest. Nothing less will content me, than *whole America.* I do not choose to consume its strength along with our own; because in all parts it is the British strength that I consume. I do not choose to be caught by a foreign enemy at the end of this exhausting conflict; and still less in the midst of it. I may escape; but I can make no insurance against such an event. Let me add, that I do not choose wholly to

break the American spirit; because it is the spirit that has made
the country.

Lastly, we have no sort of *experience* in favor of force as an in-
strument in the rule of our colonies. Their growth and their
utility has been owing to methods altogether different. Our
ancient indulgence has been said to be pursued to a fault. It
may be so. But we know, if feeling is evidence, that our fault
is more tolerable than our attempt to mend it; and our sin far
more salutary than our penitence.

These, Sir, are my reasons for not entertaining that high opinion of untried force, by which many gentlemen, for whose sentiments in other particulars I have great respect, seem to be so
greatly captivated. But there is still behind a third consideration
concerning this object, which serves to determine my opinion on
the sort of policy which ought to be pursued in the management
of America, even more than its population and its commerce.
I mean its *temper and character*.

In this character of the Americans, a love of freedom is the
predominating feature which marks and distinguishes the whole;
and as an ardent is always a jealous affection, your colonies become suspicious, restive, and untractable, whenever they see the
least attempt to wrest from them by force, or shuffle from them
by chicane, what they think the only advantage worth living for.
This fierce spirit of liberty is stronger in the English colonies,
probably, than in any other people of the earth; and this from a
great variety of powerful causes, which, to understand the true
temper of their minds, and the direction which this spirit takes, it
will not be amiss to lay open somewhat more largely.

First, the people of the colonies are descendants of Englishmen. England, Sir, is a nation which still, I hope, respects, and
formerly adored, her freedom. The colonists emigrated from you
when this part of your character was most predominant; and
they took this bias and direction the moment they parted from
your hands. They are therefore not only devoted to liberty, but
to liberty according to English ideas, and on English principles.
Abstract liberty, like other mere abstractions, is not to be found.

Liberty inheres in some sensible object; and every nation has formed to itself some favorite point which, by way of eminence, becomes the criterion of their happiness. It happened, you know, Sir, that the great contests for freedom in this country were from the earliest times chiefly upon the question of taxing. 5 Most of the contests in the ancient commonwealths turned primarily on the right of election of magistrates, or on the balance among the several orders of the state. The question of money was not with them so immediate. But in England it was otherwise. On this point of taxes the ablest pens and most eloquent 10 tongues have been exercised, the greatest spirits have acted and suffered. In order to give the fullest satisfaction concerning the importance of this point, it was not only necessary for those, who in argument defended the excellence of the English constitution, to insist on this privilege of granting money as a dry point of 15 fact, and to prove that the right had been acknowledged in ancient parchments and blind usages to reside in a certain body called a House of Commons. They went much farther; they attempted to prove, and they succeeded, that in theory it ought to be so, from the particular nature of a House of Commons as 20 an immediate representative of the people, whether the old records had delivered this oracle or not. They took infinite pains to inculcate, as a fundamental principle, that in all monarchies the people must in effect themselves, mediately or immediately,[1] possess the power of granting their own money, or no shadow 25 of liberty could subsist. The colonies draw from you, as with their lifeblood, these ideas and principles — their love of liberty, as with you, fixed and attached on this specific point of taxing. Liberty might be safe, or might be endangered, in twenty other particulars, without their being much pleased or alarmed. Here 30 they felt its pulse; and as they found that beat, they thought themselves sick or sound. I do not say whether they were right or wrong in applying your general arguments to their own case. It is not easy, indeed, to make a monopoly of theorems and corollaries. The fact is that they did thus apply those gen- 35

---

[1] " Mediately or immediately," i.e., indirectly or directly.

eral arguments; and your mode of governing them, whether through lenity or indolence, through wisdom or mistake, confirmed them in the imagination that they, as well as you, had an interest in these common principles.

5 They were further confirmed in this pleasing error by the form of their provincial legislative assemblies. Their governments are popular in a high degree. Some are merely popular; in all, the popular representative is the most weighty; and this share of the people in their ordinary government never fails to inspire 10 them with lofty sentiments, and with a strong aversion from whatever tends to deprive them of their chief importance.

If anything were wanting to this necessary operation of the form of government, religion would have given it a complete effect. Religion, always a principle of energy, in this new people 15 is no way worn out or impaired; and their mode of professing it is also one main cause of this free spirit. The people are Protestants, and of that kind which is the most adverse to all implicit submission of mind and opinion. This is a persuasion not only favorable to liberty, but built upon it. I do not think, Sir, that 20 the reason of this averseness in the dissenting churches, from all that looks like absolute government, is so much to be sought in their religious tenets as in their history. Every one knows that the Roman Catholic religion is at least coeval with most of the governments where it prevails; that it has generally gone hand 25 in hand with them, and received great favor and every kind of support from authority. The Church of England, too, was formed from her cradle under the nursing care of regular government. But the dissenting interests have sprung up in direct opposition to all the ordinary powers of the world, and could justify 30 that opposition only on a strong claim to natural liberty. Their very existence depended on the powerful and unremitted assertion of that claim. All Protestantism, even the most cold and passive, is a sort of dissent. But the religion most prevalent in our northern colonies is a refinement on the principle of resist- 35 ance; it is the dissidence of dissent,[1] and the Protestantism of

---

1 "Dissidence of dissent," i.e., the very essence of dissent.

the Protestant religion. This religion, under a variety of denominations agreeing in nothing but in the communion of the spirit of liberty, is predominant in most of the northern provinces, where the Church of England, notwithstanding its legal rights, is in reality no more than a sort of private sect, not composing, most probably, the tenth of the people. The colonists left England when this spirit was high, and in the emigrants was the highest of all; and even that stream of foreigners which has been constantly flowing into these colonies has, for the greatest part, been composed of dissenters from the establishments of their several countries, and they have brought with them a temper and character far from alien to that of the people with whom they mixed. Sir, I can perceive by their manner that some gentlemen object to the latitude of this description, because in the southern colonies the Church of England forms a large body, and has a regular establishment. It is certainly true. There is, however, a circumstance attending these colonies which, in my opinion, fully counterbalances this difference, and makes the spirit of liberty still more high and haughty than in those to the northward. It is that in Virginia and in the Carolinas they have a vast multitude of slaves. Where this is the case in any part of the world, those who are free are by far the most proud and jealous of their freedom. Freedom is to them not only an enjoyment, but a kind of rank and privilege. Not seeing there that freedom, as in countries where it is a common blessing and as broad and general as the air, may be united with much abject toil, with great misery, with all the exterior of servitude, liberty looks amongst them like something that is more noble and liberal. I do not mean, Sir, to commend the superior morality of this sentiment, which has at least as much pride as virtue in it; but I cannot alter the nature of man. The fact is so; and these people of the southern colonies are much more strongly, and with a higher and more stubborn spirit, attached to liberty than those to the northward. Such were all the ancient commonwealths; such were our Gothic[1] an-

---

1 The ancestors of the English were the Angles and not the Goths; both were Teutonic tribes.

cestors; such in our days were the Poles;[1] and such will be all masters of slaves who are not slaves themselves. In such a people the haughtiness of domination combines with the spirit of freedom, fortifies it, and renders it invincible.

5   Permit me, Sir, to add another circumstance in our colonies, which contributes no mean part toward the growth and effect of this untractable spirit. I mean their education. In no country perhaps in the world is the law so general a study. The profession itself is numerous and powerful; and in most provinces it
10 takes the lead. The greater number of the deputies sent to the Congress[2] were lawyers. But all who read—and most do read—endeavor to obtain some smattering in that science. I have been told by an eminent bookseller, that in no branch of his business, after tracts of popular devotion, were so many books as those on
15 the law exported to the plantations. The colonists have now fallen into the way of printing them for their own use. I hear that they have sold nearly as many of Blackstone's "Commentaries"[3] in America as in England. General Gage[4] marks out this disposition very particularly in a letter on your table. He states
20 that all the people in his government are lawyers, or smatterers in law; and that in Boston they have been enabled, by successful chicane, wholly to evade many parts of one of your capital penal constitutions.

The smartness of debate will say that this knowledge ought to
25 teach them more clearly the rights of legislature, their obligation to obedience, and the penalties of rebellion. All this is mighty well. But my honorable and learned friend[5] on the floor, who

1 There were but two classes in Poland, nobles and serfs. The nobles had been struggling for freer institutions, but the partition of Poland between Austria, Germany, and Russia in 1772 had defeated their hopes.

2 The First Colonial Congress, which met in Philadelphia in September, 1774.

3 Sir William Blackstone (1723–1780) wrote Commentaries on the Laws of England, a work extensively used by students of law. Its popularity is due largely to the clearness and perfection of its style.

4 Then commander of the British troops in Boston.

5 The attorney-general, Thurlow.

condescends to mark what I say for animadversion, will disdain
that ground. He has heard, as well as I, that when great honors
and emoluments do not win over this knowledge to the service
of the state, it is a formidable adversary to government. If the
spirit be not tamed and broken by these happy methods, it is stub- 5
born and litigious. *Abeunt studia in mores.*[1] This study renders
men acute, inquisitive, dexterous, prompt in attack, ready in defense, full of resources. In other countries, the people, more
simple and of a less mercurial cast, judge of an ill principle in
government only by an actual grievance; here they anticipate the 10
evil, and judge of the pressure of the grievance by the badness of
the principle. They augur misgovernment at a distance, and snuff
the approach of tyranny in every tainted breeze.

The last cause of this disobedient spirit in the colonies is
hardly less powerful than the rest, as it is not merely moral, but 15
laid deep in the natural constitution of things. Three thousand
miles of ocean lie between you and them. No contrivance can
prevent the effect of this distance in weakening government.
Seas roll and months pass between the order and the execution;
and the want of a speedy explanation of a single point is enough 20
to defeat a whole system. You have, indeed, winged ministers of
vengeance,[2] who carry your bolts in their pounces[3] to the remotest
verge of the sea. But there a power steps in, that limits the ar-
rogance of raging passions and furious elements, and says, "So
far shalt thou go, and no further."[4] Who are you, that should 25
fret and rage, and bite the chains of nature? Nothing worse
happens to you than does to all nations who have extensive empire; and it happens in all the forms into which empire can be
thrown. In large bodies, the circulation of power must be less
vigorous at the extremities. Nature has said it. The Turk can- 30
not govern Egypt, and Arabia, and Kurdistan,[5] as he governs

---

1 "Pursuits become habits." See Ovid, Heroides, xv. 83.
2 Warships.   3 Talons.
4 See Job xxxviii. 11, "Hitherto shalt thou come, but no further."
5 A country in western Asia, belonging partly to Persia and partly to
Turkey.

Thrace; nor has he the same dominion in Crimea and Algiers, which he has at Brusa[1] and Smyrna. Despotism itself is obliged to truck and huckster.[2] The Sultan gets such obedience as he can. He governs with a loose rein, that he may govern at all; and the whole of the force and vigor of his authority in his center is derived from a prudent relaxation in all his borders. Spain, in her provinces, is, perhaps, not so well obeyed as you are in yours. She complies, too; she submits; she watches times. This is the immutable condition, the eternal law, of extensive and detached empire.

Then, Sir, from these six capital sources,— of descent, of form of government, of religion in the northern provinces, of manners in the southern, of education, of the remoteness of situation from the first mover of government,—from all these causes a fierce spirit of liberty has grown up. It has grown with the growth of the people in your colonies, and increased with the increase of their wealth; a spirit that, unhappily meeting with an exercise of power in England, which, however lawful, is not reconcilable to any ideas of liberty, much less with theirs, has kindled this flame that is ready to consume us.

I do not mean to commend either the spirit in this excess, or the moral causes which produce it. Perhaps a more smooth and accommodating spirit of freedom in them would be more acceptable to us. Perhaps ideas of liberty might be desired, more reconcilable with an arbitrary and boundless authority. Perhaps we might wish the colonists to be persuaded, that their liberty is more secure when held in trust for them by us (as their guardians during a perpetual minority), than with any part of it in their own hands. The question is, not whether their spirit deserves praise or blame, but — what, in the name of God, shall we do with it? You have before you the object, such as it is, with all its glories, with all its imperfections on its head.[3] You see the magnitude; the importance; the temper; the habits;

1 A city in Asia Minor, between Constantinople and Smyrna.
2 "Truck and huckster," i.e., resort to petty bargaining.
3 See Shakespeare, Hamlet, act i, sc. 5.

the disorders. By all these considerations we are strongly urged
to determine something concerning it. We are called upon to
fix some rule and line for our future conduct, which may give a
little stability to our politics, and prevent the return of such unhappy deliberations as the present. Every such return will bring 5
the matter before us in a still more untractable form. For what
astonishing and incredible things have we not seen already!
What monsters have not been generated from this unnatural contention! Whilst every principle of authority and resistance has
been pushed, upon both sides, as far as it would go, there is no- 10
thing so solid and certain, either in reasoning or in practice, that
has not been shaken.

Until very lately, all authority in America seemed to be nothing
but an emanation from yours. Even the popular part of the colony constitution derived all its activity and its first vital movement 15
from the pleasure of the Crown. We thought, Sir, that the utmost which the discontented colonists could do, was to disturb
authority; we never dreamt they could of themselves supply it,
knowing in general what an operose business it is to establish a
government absolutely new. But having, for our purposes in this 20
contention, resolved that none but an obedient assembly should
sit, the humors of the people there, finding all passage through
the legal channel stopped, with great violence broke out another
way. Some provinces have tried their experiment, as we have
tried ours; and theirs has succeeded. They have formed a gov- 25
ernment sufficient for its purposes, without the bustle of a revolution or the troublesome formality of an election. Evident necessity and tacit consent have done the business in an instant. So
well they have done it, that Lord Dunmore[1] (the account is
among the fragments on your table) tells you that the new insti- 30
tution is infinitely better obeyed than the ancient government ever
was in its most fortunate periods. Obedience is what makes government, and not the names by which it is called; not the name
of governor, as formerly, or committee, as at present. This new
government has originated directly from the people, and was not 35

[1] Then governor of Virginia.

transmitted through any of the ordinary artificial media of a posi-
tive constitution.   It was not a manufacture ready formed, and
transmitted to them in that condition from England.   The evil
arising from hence is this : that the colonists, having once found
5 the possibility of enjoying the advantages of order in the midst of
a struggle for liberty, such struggles will not henceforward seem
so terrible to the settled and sober part of mankind as they had
appeared before the trial.

Pursuing the same plan of punishing by the denial of the exer-
10 cise of government to still greater lengths, we wholly abrogated
the ancient government of Massachusetts.[1]   We were confident
that the first feeling, if not the very prospect of anarchy, would
instantly enforce a complete submission.   The experiment was
tried.   A new, strange, unexpected face of things appeared.
15 Anarchy is found tolerable.   A vast province has now subsisted—
and subsisted in a considerable degree of health and vigor—for
near a twelvemonth, without governor, without public council,
without judges, without executive magistrates.   How long it will
continue in this state, or what may arise out of this unheard-of
20 situation, how can the wisest of us conjecture ?   Our late experience has taught us, that many of those fundamental principles,
formerly believed infallible, are either not of the importance they
were imagined to be; or that we have not at all adverted to some
other far more important and far more powerful principles, which
25 entirely overrule those we had considered as omnipotent.   I am
much against any further experiments which tend to put to the
proof any more of these allowed opinions which contribute so
much to the public tranquillity.   In effect, we suffer as much at
home by this loosening of all ties, and this concussion of all estab-
30 lished opinions, as we do abroad.   For, in order to prove that the
Americans have no right to their liberties, we are every day en-
deavoring to subvert the maxims which preserve the whole spirit

---

[1] In 1774, acts were passed by Parliament transferring to the king the
appointment of all judges and administrative officers in the colony of Massachusetts, and forbidding the holding of town meetings without the consent of
the governor.

of our own. To prove that the Americans ought not to be free, we are obliged to depreciate the value of freedom itself; and we never seem to gain a paltry advantage over them in debate, without attacking some of those principles, or deriding some of those feelings, for which our ancestors have shed their blood.   5

But, Sir, in wishing to put an end to pernicious experiments, I do not mean to preclude the fullest inquiry. Far from it! Far from deciding on a sudden or partial view, I would patiently go round and round the subject, and survey it minutely in every possible aspect. Sir, if I were capable of engaging you to an 10 equal attention, I would state that, as far as I am capable of discerning, there are but three ways of proceeding relative to this stubborn spirit which prevails in your colonies and disturbs your government. These are: to change that spirit, as inconvenient, by removing the causes; to prosecute it as criminal; or to 15 comply with it as necessary. I would not be guilty of an imperfect enumeration; I can think of but these three. Another has indeed been started — that of giving up the colonies; but it met so slight a reception that I do not think myself obliged to dwell a great while upon it. It is nothing but a little sally of anger, like 20 the frowardness of peevish children, who, when they cannot get all they would have, are resolved to take nothing.

The first of these plans,— to change the spirit as inconvenient by removing the causes, — I think, is the most like a systematic proceeding. It is radical in its principle; but it is attended with 25 great difficulties, some of them little short, as I conceive, of impossibilities. This will appear by examining into the plans which have been proposed.

As the growing population in the colonies is evidently one cause of their resistance, it was, last session, mentioned in both 30 Houses, by men of weight, and received not without applause, that in order to check this evil it would be proper for the Crown to make no further grants of land. But to this scheme there are two objections. The first, that there is already so much unsettled land in private hands as to afford room for an immense future 35 population, although the Crown not only withheld its grants but

annihilated its soil. If this be the case, then the only effect of
this avarice of desolation, this hoarding of a royal wilderness,
would be to raise the value of the possessions in the hands of the
great private monopolists, without any adequate check to the
growing and alarming mischief of population.

But if you stopped your grants, what would be the consequence? The people would occupy without grants. They have
already so occupied in many places. You cannot station garri-
sons in every part of these deserts. If you drive the people from
one place, they will carry on their annual tillage, and remove with
their flocks and herds to another. Many of the people in the
back settlements are already little attached to particular situations.
Already they have topped the Appalachian mountains. From
thence they behold before them an immense plain — one vast,
rich, level meadow, a square of five hundred miles. Over this
they would wander without a possibility of restraint; they would
change their manners with the habits of their life; would soon
forget a government by which they were disowned; would become
hordes of English Tartars,[1] and, pouring down upon your unfor-
tified frontiers a fierce and irresistible cavalry, become masters of
your governors and your counselors, your collectors and comp-
trollers, and of all the slaves that adhered to them. Such would,
and, in no long time, must be, the effect of attempting to forbid
as a crime, and to suppress as an evil, the command and blessing
of Providence, "Increase and multiply."[2] Such would be the
happy result of an endeavor to keep as a lair of wild beasts that
earth which God, by an express charter, has given to the children
of men.[3] Far different, and surely much wiser, has been our
policy hitherto. Hitherto we have invited our people, by every
kind of bounty, to fixed establishments. We have invited the
husbandman to look to authority for his title. We have taught
him piously to believe in the mysterious virtue of wax and parch-

---

[1] The Tartars were a fierce Mongol tribe, which invaded Russia in Europe
in the thirteenth century.

[2] See Gen. i. 22.

[3] See Ps. cxv. 16.

ment.[1] We have thrown each tract of land, as it was peopled, into districts, that the ruling power should never be wholly out of sight. We have settled all we could; and we have carefully attended every settlement with government.

Adhering, Sir, as I do, to this policy, as well as for the reasons I have just given, I think this new project of hedging in population to be neither prudent nor practicable.

To impoverish the colonies in general, and in particular to arrest the noble course of their marine enterprises, would be a more easy task. I freely confess it. We have shown a disposition to a system of this kind; a disposition even to continue the restraint after the offense, looking on ourselves as rivals to our colonies, and persuaded that of course we must gain all that they shall lose. Much mischief we may certainly do. The power inadequate to all other things is often more than sufficient for this. I do not look on the direct and immediate power of the colonies to resist our violence as very formidable. In this, however, I may be mistaken. But when I consider that we have colonies for no purpose but to be serviceable to us, it seems to my poor understanding a little preposterous to make them unserviceable in order to keep them obedient. It is, in truth, nothing more than the old and (as I thought) exploded problem of tyranny, which proposes to beggar its subjects into submission. But remember, when you have completed your system of impoverishment, that nature still proceeds in her ordinary course; that discontent will increase with misery; and that there are critical moments in the fortune of all states, when they who are too weak to contribute to your prosperity may be strong enough to complete your ruin. *Spoliatis arma supersunt.*[2]

The temper and character which prevail in our colonies are, I am afraid, unalterable by any human art. We cannot, I fear, falsify the pedigree of this fierce people, and persuade them that they are not sprung from a nation in whose veins the blood of freedom circulates. The language in which they would hear you

---

1 " Wax and parchment," i. e., legal procedure.

2 " Though plundered they yet have arms." See Juvenal, Sat. viii.

tell them this tale would detect the imposition; your speech would betray you. An Englishman is the unfittest person on earth to argue another Englishman into slavery.

I think it is nearly as little in our power to change their republican religion as their free descent, or to substitute the Roman Catholic as a penalty, or the Church of England as an improvement. The mode of inquisition and dragooning [1] is going out of fashion in the Old World; and I should not confide much to their efficacy in the New. The education of the Americans is also on the same unalterable bottom with their religion. You cannot persuade them to burn their books of curious science, to banish their lawyers from their courts of laws, or to quench the lights of their assemblies by refusing to choose those persons who are best read in their privileges. It would be no less impracticable to think of wholly annihilating the popular assemblies in which these lawyers sit. The army by which we must govern in their place would be far more chargeable to us; not quite so effectual, and perhaps in the end full as difficult to be kept in obedience.

With regard to the high aristocratic spirit of Virginia and the southern colonies it has been proposed, I know, to reduce it by declaring a general enfranchisement of their slaves. This project has had its advocates and panegyrists, yet I never could argue myself into any opinion of it. Slaves are often much attached to their masters. A general wild offer of liberty would not always be accepted. History furnishes few instances of it. It is sometimes as hard to persuade slaves to be free as it is to compel freemen to be slaves; and in this auspicious scheme we should have both these pleasing tasks on our hands at once. But when we talk of enfranchisement, do we not perceive that the American master may enfranchise too, and arm servile hands in defense of freedom? — a measure to which other people have had recourse more than once, and not without success, in a desperate situation of their affairs.

[1] One device for persecuting the Protestants in France in the reign of Louis XIV was to quarter upon them dragoons, who were instructed to annoy them in every conceivable way.

Slaves as these unfortunate black people are, and dull as all men are from slavery, must they not a little suspect the offer of freedom from that very nation, which has sold them to their present masters; from that nation, one of whose causes of quarrel with those masters is their refusal to deal any more in that inhuman traffic? An offer of freedom from England would come rather oddly, shipped to them in an African vessel, which is refused an entry into the ports of Virginia or Carolina, with a cargo of three hundred Angola [1] negroes. It would be curious to see the Guinea captain attempting at the same instant to publish his proclamation of liberty, and to advertise his sale of slaves. [2]

But let us suppose all these moral difficulties got over. The ocean remains. You cannot pump this dry; and as long as it continues in its present bed, so long all the causes which weaken authority by distance will continue. "Ye gods, annihilate but space and time, and make two lovers happy!" [3] was a pious and passionate prayer; but just as reasonable as many of the serious wishes of very grave and solemn politicians.

If, then, Sir, it seems almost desperate to think of any alterative course for changing the moral causes (and not quite easy to remove the natural) which produce prejudices irreconcilable to the late exercise of our authority, — but that the spirit infallibly will continue, and, continuing, will produce such effects as now embarrass us,— the second mode under consideration is to prosecute that spirit in its overt acts as *criminal*.

At this proposition I must pause a moment. The thing seems a great deal too big for my ideas of jurisprudence. It should seem to my way of conceiving such matters, that there is a very wide difference in reason and policy between the mode of proceeding on the irregular conduct of scattered individuals, or even

[1] A colony belonging to Portugal, on the west coast of Africa, formerly famous for its extensive slave trade.

[2] Though the employment of slaves in England had been forbidden by a law enacted in 1772, the English nation continued to carry on a very lucrative trade, in negroes imported from Africa, with the American colonies.

[3] From one of Dryden's plays.

of bands of men, who disturb order within the state, and the civil dissensions which may from time to time, on great questions, agitate the several communities which compose a great empire. It looks to me to be narrow and pedantic to apply the ordinary ideas of criminal justice to this great public contest. I do not know the method of drawing up an indictment against a whole people. I cannot insult and ridicule the feelings of millions of my fellow creatures as Sir Edward Coke[1] insulted one excellent individual (Sir Walter Raleigh) at the bar. I hope I am not ripe to pass sentence on the gravest public bodies, intrusted with magistracies of great authority and dignity, and charged with the safety of their fellow citizens upon the very same title that I am. I really think that for wise men this is not judicious; for sober men, not decent; for minds tinctured with humanity, not mild and merciful.

Perhaps, Sir, I am mistaken in my idea of an empire, as distinguished from a single state or kingdom. But my idea of it is this: that an empire is the aggregate of many states under one common head, whether this head be a monarch or a presiding republic. It does, in such constitutions, frequently happen (and nothing but the dismal, cold, dead uniformity of servitude can prevent its happening) that the subordinate parts have many local privileges and immunities. Between these privileges and the supreme common authority the line may be extremely nice. Of course disputes — often, too, very bitter disputes — and much ill blood will arise. But though every privilege is an exemption (in the case) from the ordinary exercise of the supreme authority, it is no denial of it. The claim of a privilege seems rather, *ex vi termini*,[2] to imply a superior power. For to talk of the privileges of a state, or of a person, who has no superior, is hardly any better than speaking nonsense. Now, in such unfortunate quarrels among the component parts of a great political union of com-

---

[1] A noted lawyer (1552–1634), the greatest of his day. He was harsh and violent in his manner, and, in the trial of Sir Walter Raleigh, treated the prisoner with marked discourtesy.

[2] By the meaning, or force, of the expression.

munities, I can scarcely conceive anything more completely im-
prudent than for the head of the empire to insist that, if any privilege is pleaded against his will or his acts, his whole authority
is denied; instantly to proclaim rebellion, to beat to arms, and to
put the offending provinces under the ban. Will not this, Sir, 5
very soon teach the provinces to make no distinctions on their
part? Will it not teach them that the government, against which
a claim of liberty is tantamount to high treason, is a government
to which submission is equivalent to slavery? It may not always
be quite convenient to impress dependent communities with such 10
an idea.

We are, indeed, in all disputes with the colonies, by the necessity of things, the judge. It is true, Sir. But I confess that the
character of judge in my own cause is a thing that frightens me.
Instead of filling me with pride, I am exceedingly humbled by it. 15
I cannot proceed with a stern, assured, judicial confidence, until
I find myself in something more like a judicial character. I
must have these hesitations as long as I am compelled to recollect that, in my little reading upon such contests as these, the
sense of mankind has, at least, as often decided against the su- 20
perior as the subordinate power. Sir, let me add, too, that the
opinion of my having some abstract right in my favor would not
put me much at my ease in passing sentence, unless I could be
sure that there were no rights which, in their exercise under certain circumstances, were not the most odious of all wrongs, and 25
the most vexatious of all injustice. Sir, these considerations
have great weight with me, when I find things so circumstanced
that I see the same party, at once a civil litigant against me in
point of right, and a culprit before me; while I sit as a criminal
judge on acts of his, whose moral quality is to be decided upon 30
the merits of that very litigation. Men are every now and then
put, by the complexity of human affairs, into strange situations;
but justice is the same, let the judge be in what situation he will.

There is, Sir, also a circumstance which convinces me that this
mode of criminal proceeding is not (at least in the present stage 35
of our contest) altogether expedient; which is nothing less than

the conduct of those very persons who have seemed to adopt that mode, by lately declaring a rebellion in Massachusetts Bay, as they had formerly addressed to have traitors brought hither, under an act of Henry VIII [1] for trial.   For though rebellion is declared, it is not proceeded against as such; nor have any steps been taken toward the apprehension or conviction of any individual offender, either on our late or our former address; but modes of public coercion have been adopted, and such as have much more resemblance to a sort of qualified hostility toward an independent power than the punishment of rebellious subjects. All this seems rather inconsistent; but it shows how difficult it is to apply these juridical ideas to our present case.

In this situation, let us seriously and coolly ponder.   What is it we have got by all our menaces, which have been many and ferocious?   What advantage have we derived from the penal laws we have passed, and which, for the time, have been severe and numerous?   What advances have we made toward our object, by the sending of a force, which, by land and sea, is no contemptible strength?   Has the disorder abated?   Nothing less. [2] When I see things in this situation, after such confident hopes, bold promises, and active exertions, I cannot, for my life, avoid a suspicion that the plan itself is not correctly right.

If, then, the removal of the causes of this spirit of American liberty be, for the greater part, or rather entirely, impracticable; if the ideas of criminal process be inapplicable, or if applicable, are in the highest degree inexpedient, what way yet remains? No way is open but the third and last — to comply with the American spirit as necessary; or, if you please, to submit to it as a necessary evil.

If we adopt this mode, if we mean to conciliate and concede, let us see of what nature the concession ought to be.   To ascertain the nature of our concession, we must look at their complaint. The colonies complain that they have not the characteristic mark and seal of British freedom.   They complain that they are

---

[1] King of England from 1509 to 1547.

[2] "Nothing less," i.e., nothing has abated less.

taxed in a Parliament in which they are not represented. If you mean to satisfy them at all, you must satisfy them with regard to this complaint. If you mean to please any people, you must give them the boon which they ask; not what you may think better for them, but of a kind totally different. Such an act may be a wise regulation, but it is no concession ; whereas our present theme is the mode of giving satisfaction.

Sir, I think you must perceive that I am resolved this day to have nothing at all to do with the question of the right of taxation. Some gentlemen startle — but it is true; I put it totally out of the question. It is less than nothing in my consideration. I do not indeed wonder, nor will you, Sir, that gentlemen of profound learning are fond of displaying it on this profound subject. But my consideration is narrow, confined, and wholly limited to the policy of the question. I do not examine whether the giving away a man's money be a power excepted and reserved out of the general trust of government; and how far all mankind, in all forms of polity, are entitled to an exercise of that right by the charter of nature. Or whether, on the contrary, a right of taxation is necessarily involved in the general principle of legislation, and inseparable from the ordinary supreme power. These are deep questions, where great names militate against each other, where reason is perplexed, and an appeal to authorities only thickens the confusion. For high and reverend authorities lift up their heads on both sides, and there is no sure footing in the middle. This point is the great

> Serbonian bog,
> 'Twixt Damiata and Mount Cassius old,
> Where armies whole have sunk.[1]

I do not intend to be overwhelmed in that bog, though in such respectable company.

---

[1] See Milton, Paradise Lost, Book ii, lines 592, 593. Lake Serbonis was surrounded by high hills of sand, which was often carried into the water by violent winds, and floated on the surface, giving the lake a solid appearance. Herodotus and Diodorus Siculus speak of armies that had disappeared in its depths.

4

The question with me is, not whether you have a right to render your people miserable, but whether it is not your interest to make them happy. It is not what a lawyer tells me I *may* do; but what humanity, reason, and justice tell me I ought to do. Is a politic act the worse for being a generous one? Is no concession proper but that which is made from your want of right to keep what you grant? Or does it lessen the grace or dignity of relaxing in the exercise of an odious claim, because you have your evidence room full of titles, and your magazines stuffed with arms to enforce them? What signify all those titles, and all those arms? Of what avail are they, when the reason of the thing tells me that the assertion of my title is the loss of my suit, and that I could do nothing but wound myself by the use of my own weapons?

Such is steadfastly my opinion of the absolute necessity of keeping up the concord of this empire by a unity of spirit, though in a diversity of operations, that, if I were sure the colonists had, at their leaving this country, sealed a regular compact of servitude; that they had solemnly abjured all the rights of citizens; that they had made a vow to renounce all ideas of liberty for them and their posterity to all generations; yet I should hold myself obliged to conform to the temper I found universally prevalent in my own day, and to govern two millions of men, impatient of servitude, on the principles of freedom. I am not determining a point of law; I am restoring tranquillity; and the general character and situation of a people must determine what sort of government is fitted for them. That point nothing else can or ought to determine.

My idea, therefore, without considering whether we yield as matter of right, or grant as matter of favor, is *to admit the people of our colonies into an interest in the constitution;* and, by recording that admission in the journals of Parliament, to give them as strong an assurance as the nature of the thing will admit, that we mean forever to adhere to that solemn declaration of systematic indulgence.

Some years ago, the repeal of a revenue act, upon its understood principle, might have served to show that we intended an unconditional abatement of the exercise of a taxing power. Such a measure was then sufficient to remove all suspicion, and to give perfect content. But unfortunate events since that time may make something further necessary; and not more necessary for the satisfaction of the colonies than for the dignity and con- 5 sistency of our own future proceedings.

I have taken a very incorrect measure of the disposition of the House, if this proposal in itself would be received with dislike. I think, Sir, we have few American financiers. But our misfortune is, we are too acute; we are too exquisite in our conjectures of 10 the future, for men oppressed with such great and present evils. The more moderate among the opposers of parliamentary conces- sion freely confess that they hope no good from taxation; but they apprehend the colonists have further views, and, if this point were conceded, they would instantly attack the trade laws. 15 These gentlemen are convinced that this was the intention from the beginning, and the quarrel of the Americans with taxation was no more than a cloak and cover to this design. Such has been the language even of a gentleman of real moder- ation, and of a natural temper well adjusted to fair and equal 20 government. I am, however, Sir, not a little surprised at this kind of discourse, whenever I hear it; and I am the more sur- prised, on account of the arguments which I constantly find in company with it, and which are often urged from the same mouths, and on the same day. 25

For instance, when we allege that it is against reason to tax a people under so many restraints in trade as the Americans, the noble lord in the blue riband shall tell you that the restraints on trade are futile and useless, of no advantage to us, and of no burthen to those on whom they are imposed; that the trade to 30 America is not secured by the acts of navigation, but by the natural and irresistible advantage of a commercial preference. Such is the merit of the trade laws in this posture of the de- bate. But when strong internal circumstances are urged against the taxes, when the scheme is dissected, when experience and 35 the nature of things are brought to prove (and do prove) the utter impossibility of obtaining an effective revenue from the colonies,—when these things are pressed, or rather press themselves, so as to drive the advocates of colony taxes to a clear admission of the futility of the scheme,—then, Sir, the sleeping trade laws revive from their trance; and this useless taxation is to be kept sacred, not for its own sake, but as a counter-guard and security of the laws of trade.

Then, Sir, you keep up revenue laws which are mischievous, in order to preserve trade laws that are useless. Such is the wisdom of our plan in both its members. They are separately given up as of no value; and yet one is always to be defended for the sake of the other. But I cannot agree with the noble lord, nor with the pamphlet [1] from whence he seems to have borrowed these ideas concerning the inutility of the trade laws. For, without idolizing them, I am sure they are still, in many ways, of great use to us; and in former times they have been of the greatest. They do confine, and they do greatly narrow, the market for the Americans. But my perfect conviction of this does not help me in the least to discern how the revenue laws form any security whatsoever to the commercial regulations; or that these commercial regulations are the true ground of the quarrel; or that the giving way, in any one instance, of authority is to lose all that may remain unconceded.

One fact is clear and indisputable. The public and avowed origin of this quarrel was on taxation. This quarrel has indeed brought on new disputes on new questions; but certainly the least bitter, and the fewest of all, on the trade laws. To judge which of the two be the real, radical cause of quarrel, we have to see whether the commercial dispute did, in order of time, precede the dispute on taxation? There is not a shadow of evidence for it. Next, to enable us to judge whether at this moment a dislike to the trade laws be the real cause of quarrel, it is absolutely necessary to put the taxes out of the question by

1 Written by Dr. Tucker, Dean of Gloucester, who wrote tracts on political and commercial subjects, and advocated granting the Americans independence.

a repeal. See how the Americans act in this position, and then you will be able to discern correctly what is the true object of the controversy, or whether any controversy at all will remain. Unless you consent to remove this cause of difference, it is impossible, with decency, to assert that the dispute is not upon what 5 it is avowed to be. And I would, Sir, recommend to your serious consideration, whether it be prudent to form a rule for punishing people, not on their own acts but on your conjectures? Surely it is preposterous at the very best. It is not justifying your anger by their misconduct; but it is converting your ill- 10 will into their delinquency.

But the colonies will go further. Alas! alas! When will this speculating against fact and reason end? What will quiet these panic fears which we entertain of the hostile effect of a conciliatory conduct? Is it true that no case can exist in which it is 15 proper for the sovereign to accede to the desires of his discontented subjects? Is there anything peculiar in this case, to make a rule for itself? Is all authority of course lost, when it is not pushed to the extreme? Is it a certain maxim, that the fewer causes of dissatisfaction are left by government, the more the sub- 20 ject will be inclined to resist and rebel?

All these objections being in fact no more than suspicions, conjectures, divinations, formed in defiance of fact and experience, they did not, Sir, discourage me from entertaining the idea of a conciliatory concession, founded on the principles which I have 25 just stated.

In forming a plan for this purpose, I endeavored to put myself in that frame of mind which was the most natural, and the most reasonable, and which was certainly the most probable means of securing me from all error. I set out with a perfect 30 distrust of my own abilities, a total renunciation of every speculation of my own, and with a profound reverence for the wisdom of our ancestors, who have left us the inheritance of so happy a constitution, and so flourishing an empire, and — what is a thousand times more valuable — the treasury of the maxims and prin- 35 ciples which formed the one and obtained the other.

During the reigns of the Kings of Spain of the Austrian family,[1] whenever they were at a loss in the Spanish councils, it was
common for their statesmen to say that they ought to consult
the genius of Philip II.[2] The genius of Philip II might mislead
5 them; and the issue of their affairs showed that they had not
chosen the most perfect standard. But, Sir, I am sure that I
shall not be misled, when, in a case of constitutional difficulty, I
consult the genius of the English constitution. Consulting at
that oracle (it was with all due humility and piety), I found four
10 capital examples in a similar case before me: those of Ireland,
Wales, Chester, and Durham.

Ireland, before the English conquest, though never governed
by a despotic power, had no Parliament. How far the English
Parliament itself was at that time modeled according to the
15 present form, is disputed among antiquarians. But we have all
the reason in the world to be assured that a form of Parliament,
such as England then enjoyed, she instantly communicated to
Ireland; and we are equally sure that almost every successive
improvement in constitutional liberty, as fast as it was made
20 here, was transmitted thither. The feudal baronage and the
feudal knighthood,[3] the roots of our primitive constitution, were
early transplanted into that soil, and grew and flourished there.
Magna Charta,[4] if it did not give us originally the House of
Commons, gave us at least a House of Commons of weight and

[1] Charles I of Spain, better known as Emperor Charles V of Germany,
was grandson of Ferdinand and Isabella, and succeeded his grandfather on
the throne of Spain. His mother was the daughter of Ferdinand and Isabella, but his father was Archduke of Austria, and so Charles and his descendants, who occupied the Spanish throne for nearly two hundred years, are sometimes known as the Kings of the Austrian family.

[2] King of Spain from 1556 to 1598. Spain was at that time in the height
of her prosperity.

[3] Burke here has reference to the early English system of land tenure,
government, and representation, from which the present system has been
gradually evolved. The assemblies convened by the king were made up of
nobles (who held their land as vassals of the king) and bishops.

[4] The great charter of English liberty, extorted from King John by the
barons in 1215.

consequence. But your ancestors did not churlishly sit down alone to the feast of Magna Charta. Ireland was made immediately a partaker. This benefit of English laws and liberties, I confess, was not at first extended to *all* Ireland. Mark the consequence. English authority and English liberties had exactly the same boundaries. Your standard could never be advanced an inch before your privileges. Sir John Davies[1] shows, beyond a doubt, that the refusal of a general communication of these rights was the true cause why Ireland was five hundred years in subduing; and after the vain projects of a military government, attempted in the reign of Queen Elizabeth,[2] it was soon discovered that nothing could make that country English in civility and allegiance but your laws and your forms of legislature.

It was not English arms, but the English constitution that conquered Ireland. From that time Ireland has ever had a general Parliament, as she had before a partial Parliament. You changed the people; you altered the religion; but you never touched the form or the vital substance of free government in that kingdom. You deposed kings; you restored them; you altered the succession to theirs, as well as to your own Crown; but you never altered their constitution, the principle of which was respected by usurpation, restored with the restoration of monarchy, and established, I trust, for ever, by the glorious Revolution.[3] This has made Ireland the great and flourishing kingdom that it is, and from a disgrace and a burthen intolerable to this nation, has rendered her a principal part of our strength and ornament. This country cannot be said to have ever formally taxed her. The irregular things done in the confusion of mighty troubles, and on the hinge of great revolutions, even if all were done that is said to have been done, form no example. If they have any effect

---

[1] A poet and statesman (1570–1626), who, in 1603, was made solicitor-general, and soon after attorney-general, of Ireland. A few years later he published a valuable work on the political condition of Ireland.

[2] Queen of England from 1558 to 1603.

[3] The Revolution of 1688–89 in England, in which the doctrine of the divine right of kings received its death-blow, and the supremacy of Parliament was established.

in argument, they make an exception to prove the rule. None of your own liberties could stand a moment if the casual deviations from them, at such times, were suffered to be used as proofs of their nullity. By the lucrative amount of such casual breaches
5 in the constitution, judge what the stated and fixed rule of supply has been in that kingdom. (Your Irish pensioners would starve if they had no other fund to live on than taxes granted by English authority.) Turn your eyes to those popular grants from whence all your great supplies are come, and learn to respect
10 that only source of public wealth in the British Empire.

My next example is Wales. This country was said to be reduced by Henry III.[1] It was said more truly to be so by Edward I.[2] But though then conquered, it was not looked upon as any part of the realm of England. Its old constitution, what-
15 ever that might have been, was destroyed; and no good one was substituted in its place. The care of that tract was put into the hands of lords marchers[3] — a form of government of a very singular kind, a strange heterogeneous monster, something between hostility and government; perhaps it has a sort of resemblance,
20 according to the modes of those times, to that of commander in chief at present, to whom all civil power is granted as secondary. The manners of the Welsh nation followed the genius of the government. The people were ferocious, restive, savage, and uncultivated; sometimes composed, never pacified. Wales, within itself,
25 was in perpetual disorder; and it kept the frontier of England in perpetual alarm. Benefits from it to the state there were none; Wales was only known to England by incursion and invasion.

Sir, during that state of things, Parliament was not idle. They attempted to subdue the fierce spirit of the Welsh by all sorts of
30 vigorous laws. They prohibited by statute the sending all sorts

[1] King of England from 1216 to 1272.

[2] King of England from 1272 to 1307. Wales gave allegiance to Henry III at times, when compelled to do so, but was not fully conquered until the time of Edward I.

[3]. The lords marchers were officers appointed by England to keep order in the marches, or border lands, of Wales.

of arms into Wales, as you prohibit by proclamation (with something more of doubt on the legality) the sending arms to America. They disarmed the Welsh by statute, as you attempted (but still with more question on the legality) to disarm New England by an instruction.[1] They made an act to drag offenders from Wales into England for trial, as you have done (but with more hardship) with regard to America. By another act, where one of the parties was an Englishman, they ordained that his trial should be always by English. They made acts to restrain trade, as you do; and they prevented the Welsh from the use of fairs and markets, as you do the Americans from fisheries and foreign ports. In short, when the statute book was not quite so much swelled as it is now, you find no less than fifteen acts of penal regulation on the subject of Wales.

Here we rub our hands — a fine body of precedents for the authority of Parliament and the use of it! I admit it fully; and pray add likewise to these precedents, that all the while Wales rid[2] this kingdom like an *incubus;*[3] that it was an unprofitable and oppressive burthen; and that an Englishman traveling in that country could not go six yards from the highroad without being murdered.

The march of the human mind is slow. Sir, it was not, until after two hundred years, discovered that by an eternal law Providence had decreed vexation to violence, and poverty to rapine. Your ancestors did, however, at length open their eyes to the ill-husbandry of injustice. They found that the tyranny of a free people could, of all tyrannies, the least be endured; and that laws made against a whole nation were not the most effectual methods for securing its obedience. Accordingly, in the twenty-seventh year of Henry VIII the course was entirely altered. With a preamble stating the entire and perfect rights of the Crown of England, it gave to the Welsh all the rights and privileges of English subjects. A political order was established; the mili-

1 That is, by an order to Gage, the commander in America.
2 Old form of "rode."
3 Nightmare.

tary power gave way to the civil; the marches were turned into
counties. But that a nation should have a right to English liberties, and yet no share at all in the fundamental security of these
liberties,— the grant of their own property,— seemed a thing so
5 incongruous, that eight years after, that is, in the thirty-fifth of
that reign, a complete and not ill-proportioned representation by
counties and boroughs was bestowed upon Wales by act of Parliament. From that moment, as by a charm, the tumults subsided;
obedience was restored; peace, order, and civilization followed in
10 the train of liberty. When the day-star of the English constitution had arisen in their hearts, all was harmony within and
without.

> — *Simul alba nautis*
>   *Stella refulsit,*
> 15   *Defluit saxis agitatus humor,*
>   *Concidunt venti, fugiuntque nubes,*
>   *Et minax (quod sic voluere) ponto*
>   *Unda recumbit.*[1]

The very same year the county palatine[2] of Chester received
20 the same relief from its oppressions, and the same remedy to its
disorders. Before this time Chester was little less distempered
than Wales. The inhabitants, without rights themselves, were
fittest to destroy the rights of others; and from thence Richard II[3]
drew the standing army of archers, with which for a time he op-
25 pressed England. The people of Chester applied to Parliament
in a petition penned as I shall read it to you:

1 " As soon as the clear-shining constellation has shone forth to the sailors,
the troubled surge falls down from the rocks, the winds cease, the clouds van-
ish, and the threatening waves subside in the sea,— because it was their will."
— Horace, Ode to Augustus, i. 12 (Smart's trans.).

2 A county palatine in England was so called because the owner, or holder,
was entitled to special privileges and prerogatives, like a king in his palace.
He appointed his own officers of justice, and could pardon crimes committed
within his territory. There were three counties palatine in England — Lan-
caster, Chester, and Durham, the two first-named in the eastern part, and the
last in the northern.

3 King of England from 1377 to 1399.

" To the king our sovereign lord, in most humble wise shown unto your excellent Majesty, the inhabitants of your Grace's county palatine of Chester: That where the said county palatine of Chester is and hath been always hitherto exempt, excluded and separated out and from your high court of Parliament, to have 5 any knights and burgesses within the said court; by reason whereof the said inhabitants have hitherto sustained manifold disherisons,[1] losses, and damages, as well in their lands, goods, and bodies, as in the good, civil, and politic governance and maintenance of the commonwealth of their said country: (2) And forasmuch as the 10 said inhabitants have always hitherto been bound by the acts and statutes made and ordained by your said Highness, and your most noble progenitors, by authority of the said court, as far forth as other counties, cities, and boroughs have been, that have had their knights and burgesses within your said court of Parliament, 15 and yet have had neither knight ne [2] burgess there for the said county palatine; the said inhabitants, for lack thereof, have been oftentimes touched and grieved with acts and statutes made within the said court, as well derogatory unto the most ancient jurisdic-tions, liberties, and privileges of your said county palatine, as pre- 20 judicial unto the commonwealth, quietness, rest, and peace of your Grace's most bounden subjects inhabiting within the same."

What did Parliament with this audacious address? Reject it as a libel? Treat it as an affront to government? Spurn it as a derogation from the rights of legislature? Did they toss it over 25 the table? Did they burn it by the hands of the common hang-man? They took the petition of grievance, all rugged as it was, without softening or temperament, unpurged of the original bitter-ness and indignation of complaint; they made it the very pre-amble to their act of redress, and consecrated its principle to all 30 ages in the sanctuary of legislation.

Here is my third example. It was attended with the success of the two former. Chester, civilized as well as Wales, has dem-onstrated that freedom, and not servitude, is the cure of anarchy;

[1] Acts of disinheritance; here it means deprivations.   [2] Old form of " nor."

as religion, and not atheism, is the true remedy for superstition. Sir, this pattern of Chester was followed in the reign of Charles II [1] with regard to the county palatine of Durham, which is my fourth example. This county had long lain out of the pale of free legislation. So scrupulously was the example of Chester followed, that the style of the preamble is nearly the same with that of the Chester act; and, without affecting the abstract extent of the authority of Parliament, it recognizes the equity of not suffering any considerable district, in which the British subjects may act as a body, to be taxed without their own voice in the grant.

Now, if the doctrines of policy contained in these preambles, and the force of these examples in the acts of Parliament avail anything, what can be said against applying them with regard to America? Are not the people of America as much Englishmen as the Welsh? The preamble of the act of Henry VIII says the Welsh speak a language no way resembling that of his Majesty's English subjects. Are the Americans not as numerous? If we may trust the learned and accurate Judge Barrington's account of North Wales, and take that as a standard to measure the rest, there is no comparison. The people cannot amount to above 200,000 — not a tenth part of the number in the colonies. Is America in rebellion? Wales was hardly ever free from it. Have you attempted to govern America by penal statutes? You made fifteen for Wales. But your legislative authority is perfect with regard to America; was it less perfect in Wales, Chester, and Durham? But America is virtually represented. What! Does the electric force of virtual representation more easily pass over the Atlantic than pervade Wales, which lies in your neighborhood; or than Chester and Durham, surrounded by abundance of representation that is actual and palpable? But, Sir, your ancestors thought this sort of virtual representation, however ample, to be totally insufficient for the freedom of the inhabitants of territories that are so near, and comparatively so inconsiderable. How, then, can I think it sufficient for those which are infinitely greater, and infinitely more remote?

[1] King of England from 1660 to 1685.

You will now, Sir, perhaps imagine that I am on the point of proposing to you a scheme for a representation of the colonies in Parliament. Perhaps I might be inclined to entertain some such thought; but a great flood stops me in my course. *Opposuit natura*[1]— I cannot remove the eternal barriers of the creation. The thing in that mode I do not know to be possible. As I meddle with no theory, I do not absolutely assert the impracticability of such a representation. But I do not see my way to it; and those who have been more confident have not been more successful. However, the arm of public benevolence is not shortened, and there are often several means to the same end. What nature has disjoined in one way, wisdom may unite in another. When we cannot give the benefit as we would wish, let us not refuse it altogether. If we cannot give the principal, let us find a substitute. But how? Where? What substitute?

Fortunately, I am not obliged, for the ways and means of this substitute, to tax my own unproductive invention. I am not even obliged to go to the rich treasury of the fertile framers of imaginary commonwealths — not to the "Republic" of Plato[2]; not to the "Utopia" of More[3]; not to the "Oceana" of Harrington.[4] It is before me; it is at my feet,

> And the dull swain
> Treads on it daily with his clouted shoon.[5]

1 "Nature has erected barriers."

2 A great Greek philosopher, born about 427 B. C. He was a disciple of Socrates, whose teachings he gives us in his Dialogues. His Republic is a picture of an ideal state where the most perfect justice prevails.

3 Sir Thomas More (1480-1535), an eminent philosopher and statesman. In 1516 he produced his famous work, Utopia. The name is derived from a Greek word meaning "nowhere," and the book is a description of an imaginary commonwealth, where the citizens had all things in common, and the administration of law and justice were perfect. By contrast he showed the evils of the then existing government in England. The adjective "utopian" is now applied to any visionary and impracticable scheme of reform.

4 James Harrington (1611-1677), an English writer, whose principal work, Oceana, a political allegory, describes an ideal republic supposed to represent England. The project was generally considered highly impracticable.

5 See Milton, Comus, lines 634, 635. "Clouted shoon," i.e., hobnailed shoes.

I only wish you to recognize, for the theory, the ancient constitutional policy of this kingdom with regard to representation, as that policy has been declared in acts of Parliament; and, as to the practice, to return to that mode which an uniform experience has marked out to you as best, and in which you walked with security, advantage, and honor until the year 1763.

My resolutions, therefore, mean to establish the equity and justice of a taxation of America by *grant*, and not by *imposition*; to mark the *legal competency* of the colony assemblies for the support of their government in peace, and for public aids in time of war; to acknowledge that this legal competency has had *a dutiful and beneficial exercise*, and that experience has shown the benefit of their grants and the futility of parliamentary taxation as a method of supply.

These solid truths compose six fundamental propositions. There are three more resolutions corollary to these. If you admit the first set, you can hardly reject the others. But if you admit the first, I shall be far from solicitous whether you accept or refuse the last. I think these six massive pillars will be of strength sufficient to support the temple of British concord.[1] I have no more doubt than I entertain of my existence that, if you admitted these, you would command an immediate peace, and, with but tolerable future management, a lasting obedience in America. I am not arrogant in this confident assurance. The propositions are all mere matters of fact; and if they are such facts as draw irresistible conclusions even in the stating, this is the power of truth, and not any management of mine.

Sir, I shall open the whole plan to you, together with such observations on the motions as may tend to illustrate them where they may want explanation. The first is a resolution: "That the colonies and plantations of Great Britain in North America, consisting of fourteen separate governments, and containing two millions and upwards of free inhabitants, have not had the liberty

[1] An allusion to the Temple of Concord at Rome, built at the head of the Forum. The ruins of the latest building, which was erected by the Emperor Tiberius, may still be seen.

and privilege of electing and sending any knights and burgesses, or others, to represent them in the high court of Parliament." This is a plain matter of fact, necessary to be laid down, and (excepting the description) it is laid down in the language of the constitution; it is taken nearly *verbatim* from acts of Parliament.

The second is like unto the first: "That the said colonies and plantations have been liable to, and bounden by, several subsidies, payments, rates, and taxes, given and granted by Parliament, though the said colonies and plantations have not their knights and burgesses in the said high court of Parliament, of their own election, to represent the condition of their country; by lack whereof they have been oftentimes touched and grieved by subsidies given, granted, and assented to, in the said court, in a manner prejudicial to the commonwealth, quietness, rest, and peace of the subjects inhabiting within the same."

Is this description too hot or too cold, too strong or too weak? Does it arrogate too much to the supreme legislature? Does it lean too much to the claims of the people? If it runs into any of these errors, the fault is not mine. It is the language of your own ancient acts of Parliament.

Nec meus hic sermo est, sed quæ præcepit Ofellus,
Rusticus, abnormis sapiens.[1]

It is the genuine produce of the ancient, rustic, manly, home-bred sense of this country. I did not dare to rub off a particle of the venerable rust that rather adorns and preserves than destroys the metal. It would be a profanation to touch with a tool the stones which construct the sacred altar of peace. I would not violate with modern polish the ingenuous and noble roughness of these truly constitutional materials. Above all things, I was resolved not to be guilty of tampering — the odious vice of restless and unstable minds. I put my foot in the tracks of our forefathers, where I can neither wander nor stumble. Determining to fix

---

[1] "This is no doctrine of mine, but what Ofellus the peasant, a philosopher without rules, taught me." — Horace, Sat. ii. 2 (Smart's trans.).

articles of peace, I was resolved not to be wise beyond what was written; I was resolved to use nothing else than the form of sound words, to let others abound in their own sense, and carefully to abstain from all expressions of my own. What the law has said, 5 I say. In all things else I am silent. I have no organ but for her words. This, if it be not ingenious, I am sure is safe.

There are indeed words expressive of grievance in this second resolution, which those who are resolved always to be in the right will deny to contain matter of fact, as applied to the present case, 10 although Parliament thought them true with regard to the counties of Chester and Durham. They will deny that the Americans were ever "touched and grieved" with the taxes. If they consider nothing in taxes but their weight as pecuniary impositions, there might be some pretense for this denial. But men may be sorely 15 touched and deeply grieved in their privileges, as well as in their purses. Men may lose little in property by the act which takes away all their freedom. When a man is robbed of a trifle on the highway, it is not the twopence lost that constitutes the capital outrage. This is not confined to privileges. Even ancient 20 indulgences withdrawn, without offense on the part of those who enjoyed such favors, operate as grievances.

But were the Americans, then, not touched and grieved by the taxes, in some measure, merely as taxes? If so, why were they almost all either wholly repealed or exceedingly reduced? Were 25 they not touched and grieved even by the regulating duties of the sixth [1] of George II ? [2] Else why were the duties first reduced to one third in 1764, and afterwards to a third of that third in the year 1766? Were they not touched and grieved by the Stamp Act? [3] I shall say they were, until that tax is revived. Were 30 they not touched and grieved by the duties of 1767, which were

1 Supply "act."

2 King of England from 1727 to 1760.

3 A bill proposed in Parliament by George Grenville in 1765, by which all paper bearing the government stamp in America was to be subject to a duty, and all legal documents must be written on such paper. The American colonies refused to submit to this duty, and the act was repealed in 1766.

likewise repealed, and which Lord Hillsborough tells you (for the ministry) were laid contrary to the true principle of commerce? Is not the assurance given, by that noble person, to the colonies of a resolution to lay no more taxes on them, an admission that taxes would touch and grieve them? Is not the resolution of the noble lord in the blue riband, now standing on your journals, the strongest of all proofs that parliamentary subsidies really touched and grieved them? Else why all these changes, modifications, repeals, assurances, and resolutions?

The next proposition is: "That, from the distance of the said colonies, and from other circumstances, no method hath hitherto been devised for procuring a representation in Parliament for the said colonies." This is an assertion of a fact. I go no further on the paper, though, in my private judgment, an useful representation is impossible. I am sure it is not desired by them, nor ought it be perhaps by us; but I abstain from opinions.

The fourth resolution is: "That each of the said colonies hath within itself a body, chosen in part, or in the whole, by the freemen, freeholders, or other free inhabitants thereof, commonly called the general assembly, or general court; with powers legally to raise, levy, and assess, according to the several usage of such colonies, duties and taxes towards defraying all sorts of public services.

This competence in the colony assemblies is certain. It is proved by the whole tenor of their acts of supply in all the assemblies, in which the constant style of granting is, "an aid to his Majesty;" and acts granting to the Crown have regularly, for near a century, passed the public offices without dispute. Those who have been pleased paradoxically to deny this right, holding that none but the British Parliament can grant to the Crown, are wished to look to what is done, not only in the colonies, but in Ireland, in one uniform unbroken tenor every session. Sir, I am surprised that this doctrine should come from some of the law servants of the Crown. I say, that if the Crown could be responsible, his Majesty, but certainly the ministers, and even these law officers themselves through whose hands the acts pass biennially in Ireland, or annually in the colonies, are in an habitual course of committing impeachable offenses. What habitual offenders have been all presidents of the council, all secretaries of state, all first lords of trade, all attorneys, and all solicitors general! However, they are safe, as no one impeaches them; and there is no ground of charge against them, except in their own unfounded theories.

The fifth resolution is also a resolution of fact: "That the said general assemblies, general courts, or other bodies legally qualified as aforesaid, have at sundry times freely granted several large subsidies and public aids for his Majesty's service, according to their abilities, when required thereto by letter from one of his Majesty's principal secretaries of state; and that their right to grant the same, and their cheerfulness and sufficiency in the said grants, have been at sundry times acknowledged by Parliament." To say nothing of their great expenses in the Indian wars; and not to take their exertion in foreign ones, so high as the supplies in the year 1695; not to go back to their public contributions in the year 1710: I shall begin to travel only where the journals give me light, resolving to deal in nothing but fact, authenticated by parliamentary record, and to build myself wholly on that solid basis.

On the 4th of April, 1748, a committee of this House came to the following resolution:

"Resolved,
"That it is the opinion of this committee, *That it is just and reasonable* that the several provinces and colonies of Massachusetts Bay, New Hampshire, Connecticut, and Rhode Island, be reimbursed the expenses they have been at in taking and securing to the Crown of Great Britain the island of Cape Breton and its dependencies."

These expenses were immense for such colonies. They were above £200,000 sterling — money first raised and advanced on their public credit.

On the 28th of January, 1756, a message from the king[1] came to us, to this effect:

"His Majesty, being sensible of the zeal and vigor with which his faithful subjects of certain colonies in North America have exerted themselves in defense of his Majesty's just rights and possessions, recommends it to this House to take the same into their consideration, and to enable his Majesty to give them such assistance as may be a *proper reward and encouragement.*"

On the 3d of February, 1756, the House came to a suitable resolution, expressed in words nearly the same as those of the message; but with the further addition, that the money then voted was as an *encouragement* to the colonies to exert themselves with vigor. It will not be necessary to go through all the testimonies which your own records have given to the truth of my resolutions, I will only refer you to the places in the journals:

Vol. xxvii.—16th and 19th May, 1757.
Vol. xxviii.—June 1st, 1758 — April 26th and 30th, 1759 —
    March 26th and 31st, and April 28th, 1760 —
    Jan. 9th and 20th, 1761.
Vol. xxix.—Jan. 22d and 26th, 1762 — March 14th and 17th, 1763.

Sir, here is the repeated acknowledgment of Parliament, that the colonies not only gave, but gave to satiety. This nation has formally acknowledged two things: first, that the colonies had gone beyond their abilities, Parliament having thought it necessary to reimburse them; secondly, that they had acted legally and laudably in their grants of money, and their maintenance of troops, since the compensation is expressly given as reward and encouragement. Reward is not bestowed for acts that are unlawful; and encouragement is not held out to things that deserve reprehension. My resolution, therefore, does nothing more than collect into one proposition, what is scattered through your journals. I give you nothing but your own; and you cannot refuse

[1] George II was then king.

in the gross, what you have so often acknowledged in detail.
The admission of this, which will be so honorable to them and
to you, will, indeed, be mortal,[1] to all the miserable stories by
which the passions of the misguided people have been engaged in
5 an unhappy system.   The people heard, indeed, from the beginning of these disputes, one thing continually dinned in their ears:
that reason and justice demanded that the Americans, who paid
no taxes, should be compelled to contribute.   How did that fact
of their paying nothing stand, when the taxing system began?
10 When Mr. Grenville[2] began to form his system of American
revenue, he stated in this House that the colonies were then in
debt two million six hundred thousand pounds sterling money,
and was of opinion they would discharge that debt in four years.
On this state, those untaxed people were actually subject to the
15 payment of taxes to the amount of six hundred and fifty thousand
a year.   In fact, however, Mr. Grenville was mistaken.   The
funds given for sinking the debt did not prove quite so ample as
both the colonies and he expected.   The calculation was too sanguine; the reduction was not completed till some years after, and
20 at different times in different colonies.   However, the taxes after
the war continued too great to bear any addition, with prudence
or propriety; and when the burthens imposed in consequence of
former requisitions were discharged, our tone became too high to
resort again to requisition.   No colony, since that time, ever has
25 had any requisition whatsoever made to it.

We see the sense of the Crown, and the sense of Parliament,
on the productive nature of a revenue by grant.   Now search the
same journals for the produce of the revenue by imposition —
Where is it?   Let us know the volume and the page.   What is
30 the gross, what is the net produce?   To what service is it ap-

1 Fatal.
2 Hon. George Grenville (1712-1770), who held the position of Prime Minister of England from 1763 to 1765, is noted as being the author of the Stamp
Act.   He was an able man, but self-willed and dictatorial, and the king, who
at first liked him because of his high-handed policy with the colonies, came
soon to hate him, and dismissed him from the position of his chief adviser.

plied? How have you appropriated its surplus? What, can none of the many skillful index-makers that we are now employing find any trace of it? Well, let them and that rest together. But are the journals, which say nothing of the revenue, as silent on the discontent? Oh, no! a child may find it. It is the melancholy burthen and blot of every page.

I think then I am, from those journals, justified in the sixth and last resolution, which is: "That it hath been found by experience, that the manner of granting the said supplies and aids, by the said general assemblies, hath been more agreeable to the said colonies, and more beneficial, and conducive to the public service, than the mode of giving and granting aids in Parliament, to be raised and paid in the said colonies."

This makes the whole of the fundamental part of the plan. The conclusion is irresistible. You cannot say that you were driven by any necessity to an exercise of the utmost rights of legislature. You cannot assert that you took on yourselves the task of imposing colony taxes, from the want of another legal body that is competent to the purpose of supplying the exigencies of the state without wounding the prejudices of the people. Neither is it true that the body so qualified, and having that competence, had neglected the duty.

The question now, on all this accumulated matter, is: Whether you will choose to abide by a profitable experience, or a mischievous theory; whether you choose to build on imagination, or fact; whether you prefer enjoyment, or hope; satisfaction in your subjects, or discontent?

If these propositions are accepted, everything which has been made to enforce a contrary system must, I take it for granted, fall along with it. On that ground, I have drawn the following resolution, which, when it comes to be moved, will naturally be divided in a proper manner: "That it may be proper to repeal an act, made in the seventh year of the reign of his present Majesty, intituled:[1] An act for granting certain duties in the British colonies and plantations in America; for allowing a drawback[2] of

---

[1] Another spelling of "entitled."   [2] Refund of a duty.

the duties of customs upon the exportation from this kingdom, of coffee and cocoanuts of the produce of the said colonies or plantations; for discontinuing the drawbacks payable on China earthenware exported to America; and for more effectually preventing
5 the clandestine running of goods in the said colonies and plantations. — And that it may be proper to repeal an act, made in the fourteenth year of the reign of his present Majesty, intituled: An act to discontinue, in such manner, and for such time, as are therein mentioned, the landing and discharging, lading or shipping,
10 of goods, wares, and merchandise, at the town, and within the harbor, of Boston, in the province of Massachusetts Bay, in North America. — And that it may be proper to repeal an act, made in the fourteenth year of the reign of his present Majesty, intituled: An act for the impartial administration of justice, in the cases of
15 persons questioned for any acts done by them, in the execution of the law, or for the suppression of riots and tumults, in the province of Massachusetts Bay, in New England. — And that it may be proper to repeal an act, made in the fourteenth year of the reign of his present Majesty, intituled: An act for the better regulating the
20 government of the province of Massachusetts Bay, in New England.— And, also, that it may be proper to explain and amend an act, made in the thirty-fifth year of the reign of King Henry VIII, intituled: An act for the trial of treasons committed out of the king's dominions."

25   I wish, Sir, to repeal the Boston Port Bill,[1] because (independently of the dangerous precedent of suspending the rights of the subject during the king's pleasure) it was passed, as I apprehend, with less regularity, and on more partial principles, than it ought. The corporation of Boston was not heard before it was condemned.
30 Other towns, full as guilty as she was, have not had their ports blocked up.   Even the restraining bill of the present session does not go to the length of the Boston Port Act.   The same ideas of prudence which induced you not to extend equal punishment to

---

[1] A bill proposed by Lord North in 1774, prohibiting the landing or shipping of goods at Boston, as a punishment for the rebellion of the people of Boston against the tax on tea.

equal guilt, even when you were punishing, induced me, who mean not to chastise, but to reconcile, to be satisfied with the punishment already partially inflicted.

Ideas of prudence and accommodation to circumstances prevent you from taking away the charters of Connecticut and Rhode Island, as you have taken away that of Massachusetts colony, though the Crown has far less power in the two former provinces than it enjoyed in the latter; and though the abuses have been full as great and as flagrant in the exempted as in the punished. The same reasons of prudence and accommodation have weight with me in restoring the charter of Massachusetts Bay. Besides, Sir, the act which changes the charter of Massachusetts is in many particulars so exceptionable, that if I did not wish absolutely to repeal, I would by all means desire to alter it; as several of its provisions tend to the subversion of all public and private justice. Such, among others, is the power in the governor to change the sheriff at his pleasure, and to make a new returning officer for every special cause. It is shameful to behold such a regulation standing among English laws.

The act for bringing persons accused of committing murder under the orders of government to England for trial is but temporary. That act has calculated the probable duration of our quarrel with the colonies, and is accommodated to that supposed duration. I would hasten the happy moment of reconciliation, and therefore must, on my principle, get rid of that most justly obnoxious act.

The act of Henry VIII, for the trial of treasons, I do not mean to take away, but to confine it to its proper bounds and original intention; to make it expressly for trial of treasons (and the greatest treasons may be committed) in places where the jurisdiction of the Crown does not extend.

Having guarded the privileges of local legislature, I would next secure to the colonies a fair and unbiased judicature; for which purpose, Sir, I propose the following resolution: "That, from the time when the general assembly or general court of any colony or plantation in North America shall have appointed by act of assembly, duly confirmed, a settled salary to the offices of the chief justice and other judges of the superior courts, it may be proper that the said chief justice and other judges of the superior courts of such colony shall hold his and their office and offices during their good behavior; and shall not be removed therefrom, but when the said removal shall be adjudged by his Majesty in council, upon a hearing on complaint from the general assembly, or on a complaint from the governor, or council, or the house of representatives, severally, or of the colony in which the said chief justice and other judges have exercised the said offices."

The next resolution relates to the courts of admiralty. It is this: "That it may be proper to regulate the courts of admiralty, or vice-admiralty, authorized by the fifteenth chapter of the fourth of George III, in such a manner as to make the same more commodious to those who sue, or are sued, in the said courts, and to provide for the more decent maintenance of the judges in the same."

These courts I do not wish to take away; they are in themselves proper establishments. This court is one of the capital securities of the Act of Navigation.[1] The extent of its jurisdiction, indeed, has been increased; but this is altogether as proper, and is indeed on many accounts more eligible, where new powers were wanted, than a court absolutely new. But courts incommodiously situated in effect deny justice, and a court partaking in the fruits of its own condemnation is a robber. The congress complain, and complain justly, of this grievance.

These are the three consequential propositions. I have thought of two or three more; but they come rather too near detail and to the province of executive government, which I wish Parliament always to superintend, never to assume. If the first six are granted, congruity will carry the latter three. If not, the things that remain unrepealed will be, I hope, rather unseemly encumbrances on the building than very materially detrimental to its strength and stability.

[1] This act prevented foreign ships from trading with English colonies, and only permitted trade with England in English ships or ships of the country supplying the merchandise carried.

Here, Sir, I should close; but I plainly perceive some objections remain, which I ought, if possible, to remove. The first will be that, in resorting to the doctrine of our ancestors, as contained in the preamble to the Chester act, I prove too much: that the grievance from a want of representation, stated in that preamble, goes to the whole of legislation as well as to taxation; and that the colonies, grounding themselves upon that doctrine, will apply it to all parts of legislative authority.

To this objection, with all possible deference and humility, and wishing as little as any man living to impair the smallest particle of our supreme authority, I answer, that the words are the words of Parliament, and not mine; and that all false and inconclusive inferences drawn from them are not mine; for I heartily disclaim any such inference. I have chosen the words of an act of Parliament which Mr. Grenville, surely a tolerably zealous and very judicious advocate for the sovereignty of Parliament, formerly moved to have read at your table in confirmation of his tenets. It is true that Lord Chatham [1] considered these preambles as declaring strongly in favor of his opinions. He was a no less powerful advocate for the privileges of the Americans. Ought I not from hence to presume, that these preambles are as favorable as possible to both when properly understood; favorable both to the rights of Parliament and to the privilege of the dependencies of this Crown? But, Sir, the object of grievance in my resolution I have not taken from the Chester, but from the Durham act, which confines the hardship of want of representation to the case of subsidies; and which therefore falls in exactly with the case of the colonies. But whether the unrepresented counties were *de jure*, [2] or *de facto*, [3] bound, the preambles do not accurately dis-

[1] William Pitt (1708–1778), perhaps the greatest of English statesmen. He was distinguished by great insight and breadth of view in political matters, and, previous to becoming Earl of Chatham, was almost worshiped by the English people, who called him the "Great Commoner." By accepting a peerage he sacrificed his popularity to a great extent. He was an advocate of greater freedom for the colonies, and vigorously opposed the Stamp Act.

[2] Literally, "from the law"; hence, rightly.

[3] Literally, "from the fact"; hence, really.

tinguish, nor indeed was it necessary; for, whether *de jure* or *de facto*, the legislature thought the exercise of the power of taxing, as of right, or as of fact without right, equally a grievance and equally oppressive.

5   I do not know that the colonies have, in any general way, or in any cool hour, gone much beyond the demand of immunity in relation to taxes.   It is not fair to judge of the temper or dispositions of any man, or any set of men, when they are composed and at rest, from their conduct, or their expressions, in a state of dis-
10 turbance and irritation.   It is, besides, a very great mistake to imagine that mankind follow up practically any speculative principle, either of government or of freedom, as far as it will go in argument and logical illation.

    We Englishmen stop very short of the principles upon which
15 we support any given part of our constitution, or even the whole of it together.   I could easily, if I had not already tired you, give you very striking and convincing instances of it.   This is nothing but what is natural and proper.   All government, indeed every human benefit and enjoyment, every virtue, and every prudent
20 act, is founded on compromise and barter.   We balance inconveniences; we give and take; we remit some rights that we may enjoy others; and we choose rather to be happy citizens than subtle disputants.   As we must give away some natural liberty to enjoy civil advantages, so we must sacrifice some civil liber-
25 ties for the advantages to be derived from the communion and fellowship of a great empire.   But, in all fair dealings, the thing bought must bear some proportion to the purchase paid.   None will barter away the immediate jewel of his soul.[1]   Though a great house is apt to make slaves haughty, yet it is purchasing a
30 part of the artificial importance of a great empire too dear to pay for it all essential rights, and all the intrinsic dignity of human nature.   None of us who would not risk his life rather than fall under a government purely arbitrary!   But although there are some amongst us who think our constitution wants
35 many improvements to make it a complete system of liberty,

1 See Shakespeare, Othello, act iii, sc. 3.

perhaps none who are of that opinion would think it right to aim at such improvement by disturbing his country and risking everything that is dear to him. In every arduous enterprise we consider what we are to lose as well as what we are to gain; and the more and better stake of liberty every people possess, the less 5 they will hazard in a vain attempt to make it more. These are *the cords of man.*[1] Man acts from adequate motives relative to his interest, and not on metaphysical speculations. Aristotle,[2] the great master of reasoning, cautions us, and with great weight and propriety, against this species of delusive geometrical accu- 10 racy in moral arguments as the most fallacious of all sophistry.

The Americans will have no interest contrary to the grandeur and glory of England, when they are not oppressed by the weight of it; and they will rather be inclined to respect the acts of a su- perintending legislature, when they see them the acts of that 15 power, which is itself the security, not the rival, of their secondary importance. In this assurance my mind most perfectly acquiesces, and I confess I feel not the least alarm from the discontents which are to arise from putting people at their ease; nor do I apprehend the destruction of this empire from giving, by an act of free grace 20 and indulgence, to two millions of my fellow citizens, some share of those rights upon which I have always been taught to value myself.

It is said, indeed, that this power of granting, vested in Ameri- can assemblies, would dissolve the unity of the empire; which 25 was preserved entire, although Wales and Chester and Durham were added to it. Truly, Mr. Speaker, I do not know what this unity means; nor has it ever been heard of, that I know, in the constitutional policy of this country. The very idea of subordina- tion of parts excludes this notion of simple and undivided unity. 30 England is the head; but she is not the head and the members too. Ireland has ever had from the beginning a separate, but not an independent, legislature; which, far from distracting, promoted

---

1 "The cords of man," i.e., the motives which govern men. See Hosea xi. 4: "I drew them with cords of a man, with bands of love."

2 A great Greek philosopher of the fourth century B. C.

the union of the whole. Everything was sweetly and harmoniously disposed through both islands for the conservation of English dominion and the communication of English liberties. I do not see that the same principles might not be carried into twenty islands, and with the same good effect. This is my model with regard to America, as far as the internal circumstances of the two countries are the same. I know no other unity of this empire than I can draw from its example during these periods, when it seemed to my poor understanding more united than it is now, or than it is likely to be by the present methods.

But since I speak of these methods, I recollect, Mr. Speaker, almost too late, that I promised before I finished to say something of the proposition of the noble lord[1] on the floor, which has been so lately received, and stands on your journals. I must be deeply concerned whenever it is my misfortune to continue a difference with the majority of this House. But as the reasons for that difference are my apology for thus troubling you, suffer me to state them in a very few words. I shall compress them into as small a body as I possibly can, having already debated that matter at large when the question was before the committee.

First, then, I cannot admit that proposition of a ransom by auction, because it is a mere project. It is a thing new, unheard of, supported by no experience, justified by no analogy, without example of our ancestors or root in the constitution. It is neither regular parliamentary taxation, nor colony grant. *Experimentum in corpore vili*[2] is a good rule, which will ever make me adverse to any trial of experiments on what is certainly the most valuable of all subjects — the peace of this empire.

Secondly, it is an experiment which must be fatal in the end to our constitution. For what is it but a scheme for taxing the colonies in the antechamber of the noble lord and his successors? To settle the quotas and proportions in this House is clearly impossible. You, Sir, may flatter yourself you shall sit a state auctioneer, with your hammer in your hand, and knock down to each

---

[1] The allusion is to Lord North.

[2] " Experiment should be made upon a worthless subject."

colony as it bids. But to settle (on the plan laid down by the noble lord) the true proportional payment for four or five and twenty governments, according to the absolute and the relative wealth of each, and according to the British proportion of wealth and burthen, is a wild and chimerical notion. This new taxation must, therefore, come in by the back door of the constitution. Each quota must be brought to this House ready formed; you can neither add nor alter. You must register it. You can do nothing further. For on what grounds can you deliberate either before or after the proposition? You cannot hear the counsel for all these provinces, quarreling each on its own quantity of payment, and its proportion to others. (If you should attempt it, the committee of provincial ways and means, or by whatever other name it will delight to be called, must swallow up all the time of Parliament.)

Thirdly, it does not give satisfaction to the complaint of the colonies. They complain that they are taxed without their consent; you answer that you will fix the sum at which they shall be taxed. That is, you give them the very grievance for the remedy. You tell them, indeed, that you will leave the mode to themselves. I really beg pardon: it gives me pain to mention it; but you must be sensible that you will not perform this part of the compact. For, suppose the colonies were to lay the duties, which furnished their contingent, upon the importation of your manufactures; you know you would never suffer such a tax to be laid. You know, too, that you would not suffer many other modes of taxation. So that when you come to explain yourself, it will be found that you will neither leave to themselves the quantum nor the mode, nor indeed anything. The whole is delusion from one end to the other.

Fourthly, this method of ransom by auction, unless it be *universally* accepted, will plunge you into great and inextricable difficulties. In what year of our Lord are the proportions of payments to be settled? To say nothing of the impossibility that colony agents should have general powers of taxing the colonies at their discretion, consider, I implore you, that the communication by special messages and orders between these agents and their constituents on each variation of the case, when the parties come to contend together and to dispute on their relative proportions, will be a matter of delay, perplexity, and confusion that never can have an end.

5   If all the colonies do not appear at the outcry, what is the condition of those assemblies who offer by themselves or their agents to tax themselves up to your ideas of their proportion? The refractory colonies, who refuse all composition, will remain taxed only to your old impositions, which, however grievous in prin-
10 ciple, are trifling as to production. The obedient colonies in this scheme are heavily taxed; the refractory remain unburthened. What will you do? Will you lay new and heavier taxes by Parliament on the disobedient? Pray consider in what way you can do it. You are perfectly convinced that, in the way of taxing,
15 you can do nothing but at the ports. Now suppose it is Virginia that refuses to appear at your auction, while Maryland and North Carolina bid handsomely for their ransom and are taxed to your quota, how will you put these colonies on a par? Will you tax the tobacco of Virginia? If you do, you give its death wound to
20 your English revenue at home, and to one of the very greatest articles of your own foreign trade. If you tax the import of that rebellious colony, what do you tax but your own manufactures, or the goods of some other obedient and already well-taxed colony?

    Who has said one word on this labyrinth[1] of detail which be-
25 wilders you more and more as you enter into it? Who has presented, who can present, you with a clue to lead you out of it? I think, Sir, it is impossible that you should not recollect that the colony bounds are so implicated in one another (you know it by your other experiments in the bill for prohibiting the New Eng-
30 land fishery), that you can lay no possible restraints on almost any of them which may not be presently eluded, if you do not confound the innocent with the guilty, and burthen those whom,

---

[1] The allusion here is to the labyrinth at Crete in which the monster Minotaur was kept. When Theseus entered this labyrinth to slay the Minotaur, Ariadne, the daughter of King Minos, gave him as a clew a skein of thread, by means of which he found his way out.

upon every principle, you ought to exonerate. He must be grossly ignorant of America who thinks that, without falling into this confusion of all rules of equity and policy, you can restrain any single colony, especially Virginia and Maryland, the central and most important of them all.

Let it also be considered that, either in the present confusion you settle a permanent contingent which will and must be trifling, and then you have no effectual revenue; or you change the quota at every exigency, and then on every new repartition you will have a new quarrel.

Reflect, besides, that when you have fixed a quota for every colony, you have not provided for prompt and punctual payment. Suppose one, two, five, ten years' arrears. You cannot issue a treasury extent [1] against the failing colony. You must make new Boston Port Bills, new restraining laws, new acts for dragging men to England for trial. You must send out new fleets, new armies. All is to begin again! From this day forward the empire is never to know an hour's tranquillity. An intestine fire will be kept alive in the bowels of the colonies, which one time or other must consume this whole empire. I allow, indeed, that the empire of Germany raises her revenue and her troops by quotas and contingents; but the revenue of the empire and the army of the empire is the worst revenue and the worst army in the world.

Instead of a standing revenue, you will, therefore, have a perpetual quarrel. Indeed the noble lord, who proposed this project of a ransom by auction, seemed himself to be of that opinion. His project was rather designed for breaking the union of the colonies than for establishing a revenue. He confessed he apprehended that his proposal would not be to *their taste*. I say, this scheme of disunion seems to be at the bottom of the project; for I will not suspect that the noble lord meant nothing but merely to delude the nation by an airy phantom which he never intended to realize. But whatever his views may be, as I propose the peace and union of the colonies as the very foundation of my

---

1 "Treasury extent," i.e., an order by which the lands and goods of a debtor to the Crown are seized for payment.

plan, it cannot accord with one whose foundation is perpetual discord.

Compare the two. This I offer to give you is plain and simple; the other, full of perplexed and intricate mazes. This is
5 mild; that harsh. This is found by experience effectual for its purposes; the other is a new project. This is universal; the other calculated for certain colonies only. This is immediate in its conciliatory operation; the other remote, contingent, full of hazard. Mine is what becomes the dignity of a ruling people — gra-
10 tuitous, unconditional, and not held out as matter of bargain and sale. I have done my duty in proposing it to you. I have, indeed, tired you by a long discourse; but this is the misfortune of those to whose influence nothing will be conceded, and who must win every inch of their ground by argument. You have heard
15 me with goodness. May you decide with wisdom! For my part, I feel my mind greatly disburthened by what I have done to-day. I have been the less fearful of trying your patience, because on this subject I mean to spare it altogether in future. I have this comfort, that, in every stage of the American affairs, I
20 have steadily opposed the measures that have produced the confusion, and may bring on the destruction of this empire. I now go so far as to risk a proposal of my own. If I cannot give peace to my country, I give it to my conscience.

But what (says the financier) is peace to us without money?
25 Your plan gives us no revenue. No! But it does; for it secures to the subject the power of *refusal*—the first of all revenues. Experience is a cheat, and fact a liar, if this power in the subject of proportioning his grant, or of not granting at all, has not been found the richest mine of revenue ever discovered by the
30 skill or by the fortune of man. It does not indeed vote you £152,750 : 11 : 2¾, nor any other paltry limited sum. But it gives the strong box itself, the fund, the bank, from whence only revenues can arise amongst a people sensible of freedom: *Posita luditur arca.*[1]

1 "The strong box itself is staked in playing." See Juvenal, Sat. i. An allusion to excess in gambling.

Cannot you in England; cannot you at this time of day; cannot you, a House of Commons, trust to the principle which has raised so mighty a revenue, and accumulated a debt of near 140 millions in this country? Is this principle to be true in England, and false everywhere else? Is it not true in Ireland? Has it not hitherto been true in the colonies? Why should you presume that, in any country, a body duly constituted for any function, will neglect to perform its duty, and abdicate its trust? Such a presumption would go against all governments in all modes. But, in truth, this dread of penury of supply, from a free assembly, has no foundation in nature. For first observe that, besides the desire which all men have, naturally, of supporting the honor of their own government, that sense of dignity and that security to property, which ever attend freedom, have a tendency to increase the stock of the free community. Most may be taken where most is accumulated. And what is the soil or climate where experience has not uniformly proved, that the voluntary flow of heaped-up plenty, bursting from the weight of its own rich luxuriance, has ever run with a more copious stream of revenue than could be squeezed from the dry husks of oppressed indigence, by the straining of all the politic machinery in the world?

Next, we know that parties must ever exist in a free country. We know, too, that the emulations of such parties, their contradictions, their reciprocal necessities, their hopes, and their fears, must send them all in their turns to him that holds the balance of the state. The parties are the gamesters; but government keeps the table, and is sure to be the winner in the end. When this game is played, I really think it is more to be feared that the people will be exhausted than that government will not be supplied. Whereas, whatever is got by acts of absolute power ill-obeyed because odious, or by contracts ill-kept because constrained, will be narrow, feeble, uncertain, and precarious.

Ease would recant
Vows made in pain, as violent and void. [1]

1 See Milton, Paradise Lost, Book iv, lines 96, 97.

I, for one, protest against compounding our demands; I declare against compounding, for a poor, limited sum, the immense, ever-growing, eternal debt which is due to generous government from protected freedom.   And so may I speed in the great object I 5 propose to you; as I think it would not only be an act of injustice, but would be the worst economy in the world, to compel the colonies to a sum certain, either in the way of ransom or in the way of compulsory compact.

But to clear up my ideas on this subject.   A revenue from 10 America transmitted hither!   Do not delude yourselves; you never can receive it.   No, not a shilling!   We have experience that from remote countries it is not to be expected.   If, when you attempted to extract revenue from Bengal, you were obliged to return in loan what you had taken in imposition, what can you 15 expect from North America ?   For certainly, if ever there was a country qualified to produce wealth, it is India; or an institution fit for the transmission, it is the East India Company.   America has none of these aptitudes.

If America gives you taxable objects, on which you lay your 20 duties here, and gives you, at the same time, a surplus by a foreign sale of her commodities, to pay the duties on these objects which you tax at home,[1] she has performed her part to the British revenue.   But with regard to her own internal establishments, she may, I doubt not she will, contribute in moderation.   I say 25 in moderation; for she ought not to be permitted to exhaust herself.   She ought to be reserved to a war; the weight of which, with the enemies that we are most likely to have, must be considerable in her quarter of the globe.   There she may serve you, and serve you essentially.

30 For that service, for all service, whether of revenue, trade, or empire, my trust is in her interest in the British constitution.   My hold of the colonies is in the close affection which grows from

1 According to the Navigation Laws, American products could not be exported to foreign countries direct, but had first to be sent to England, thence to be reëxported.   Duties were laid upon them in England, which were more than covered by the profits of foreign sale.

common names, from kindred blood, from similar privileges, and
equal protection. These are ties, which, though light as air, are as
strong as links of iron. Let the colonies always keep the idea
of their civil rights associated with your government; they will
cling and grapple to you, and no force under heaven will be of 5
power to tear them from their allegiance. But let it be once
understood that your government may be one thing and their
privileges another, that these two things may exist without any
mutual relation; the cement is gone, the cohesion is loosened,
and everything hastens to decay and dissolution. 10

As long as you have the wisdom to keep the sovereign authority
of this country as the sanctuary of liberty, the sacred temple consecrated to our common faith, wherever the chosen race and sons of
England worship freedom they will turn their faces towards you.
The more they multiply, the more friends you will have; the more 15
ardently they love liberty, the more perfect will be their obedience.
Slavery they can have anywhere. It is a weed that grows in every
soil. They may have it from Spain, they may have it from Prus-
sia. But, until you become lost to all feeling of your true interest
and your natural dignity, freedom they can have from none but 20
you. This is the commodity of price, of which you have the monopoly. This is the true act of navigation, which binds to you the
commerce of the colonies, and through them secures to you the
wealth of the world. Deny them this participation of freedom,
and you break that sole bond, which originally made, and must 25
still preserve, the unity of the empire.

Do not entertain so weak an imagination as that your registers
and your bonds, your affidavits and your sufferances, your cockets
and your clearances, are what form the great securities of your
commerce. Do not dream that your letters of office, and your in- 30
structions, and your suspending clauses, are the things that hold
together the great contexture of the mysterious whole. These
things do not make your government. Dead instruments, passive
tools as they are, it is the spirit of the English communion that
gives all their life and efficacy to them. It is the spirit of the 35
English constitution, which, infused through the mighty mass, per-

vades, feeds, unites, invigorates, vivifies every part of the empire, even down to the minutest member.

Is it not the same virtue which does everything for us here in England? Do you imagine, then, that it is the Land-tax Act which
5 raises your revenue; that it is the annual vote in the committee of supply which gives you your army; or that it is the mutiny bill which inspires it with bravery and discipline? No! Surely no! It is the love of the people; it is their attachment to their government from the sense of the deep stake they have in such a glorious
10 institution, which gives you your army and your navy, and infuses into both that liberal obedience without which your army would be a base rabble, and your navy nothing but rotten timber.

All this, I know well enough, will sound wild and chimerical to the profane herd of those vulgar and mechanical politicians
15 who have no place among us: a sort of people who think that nothing exists but what is gross and material; and who, therefore, far from being qualified to be directors of the great movement of empire, are not fit to turn a wheel in the machine. But to men truly initiated and rightly taught, these ruling and master princi-
20 ples which, in the opinion of such men as I have mentioned, have no substantial existence, are in truth everything, and all in all. Magnanimity in politics is not seldom the truest wisdom; and a great empire and little minds go ill together. If we are conscious of our situation, and glow with zeal to fill our place as becomes
25 our station and ourselves, we ought to auspicate [1] all our public proceedings on America with the old warning of the church, *Sursum corda!* [2] We ought to elevate our minds to the greatness of that trust to which the order of Providence has called us. By adverting to the dignity of this high calling, our ancestors have
30 turned a savage wilderness into a glorious empire; and have made the most extensive and the only honorable conquests, not by destroying, but by promoting the wealth, the number, the happiness of the human race. Let us get an American revenue as we have got an American empire. English privileges have made it all
35 that it is; English privileges alone will make it all it can be.

---

1 Inaugurate.   2 "Lift up your hearts,"—a call to prayer.

In full confidence of this unalterable truth, I now (*quod felix faustumque sit*) [1] lay the first stone of the temple of peace; and I move you,—

I. "That the colonies and plantations of Great Britain in North America, consisting of fourteen separate governments, and containing two millions and upwards of free inhabitants, have not had the liberty and privilege of electing and sending any knights and burgesses, or others, to represent them in the high court of Parliament."

II. "That the said colonies and plantations have been made liable to, and bounden by several subsidies, payments, rates, and taxes, given and granted by Parliament; though the said colonies and plantations have not their knights and burgesses, in the said high court of Parliament, of their own election, to represent the condition of their country; *by lack whereof they have been oftentimes touched and grieved by subsidies given, granted, and assented to, in the said court, in a manner prejudicial to the commonwealth, quietness, rest, and peace, of the subjects inhabiting within the same.*" [2]

III. "That, from the distance of the said colonies, and from other circumstances, no method hath hitherto been devised for procuring a representation in Parliament for the said colonies."

IV. "That each of the said colonies hath within itself a body, chosen, in part or in the whole, by the freemen, freeholders, or other free inhabitants thereof, commonly called the general assembly, or general court; with powers legally to raise, levy, and assess, according to the several usage of such colonies, duties and taxes towards defraying all sorts of public services."

V. "That the said general assemblies, general courts, or other bodies, legally qualified as aforesaid, have at sundry times freely granted several large subsidies and public aids for his Majesty's service, according to their abilities, when required

---

[1] "May it be happy and auspicious."

[2] The words in Italics, in this and the last motion, were, by an amendment that was carried, left out of the motion.

thereto by letter from one of his Majesty's principal secretaries of state; and that their right to grant the same, and their cheerfulness and sufficiency in the said grants, have been at sundry times acknowledged by Parliament."

5   VI. "That it hath been found by experience, that the manner of granting the said supplies and aids, by the said general assemblies, hath been more agreeable to the inhabitants of the said colonies, and more beneficial and conducive to the public service, than the mode of giving and granting aids and subsidies in Parliament to be raised and paid in the said colonies."

VII. "That it may be proper to repeal an act, made in the seventh year of the reign of his present Majesty, intituled: An act for granting certain duties in the British colonies and plantations in America; for allowing a drawback of the duties of customs, upon the exportation from this kingdom, of coffee and cocoanuts of the produce of the said colonies or plantations; for discontinuing the drawbacks payable on China earthenware exported to America; and for more effectually preventing the clandestine running of goods in the said colonies and plantations."

VIII. "That it may be proper to repeal an act, made in the fourteenth year of the reign of his present Majesty, intituled: An act to discontinue, in such manner and for such time as are therein mentioned, the landing and discharging, lading or shipping of goods, wares, and merchandise, at the town, and within the harbor, of Boston, in the province of Massachusetts Bay, in North America."

IX. "That it may be proper to repeal an act, made in the fourteenth year of the reign of his present Majesty, intituled: An act for the impartial administration of justice, in the cases of persons questioned for any acts done by them, in the execution of the law, or for the suppression of riots and tumults, in the province of Massachusetts Bay, in New England."

X. "That it is proper to repeal an act, made in the fourteenth year of the reign of his present Majesty, intituled: An act for the better regulating the government of the province of Massachusetts Bay, in New England."

XI. "That it is proper to explain and amend an act made in the thirty-fifth year of the reign of King Henry VIII, intituled: An act for the trial of treasons committed out of the king's dominions."

XII. "That, from the time when the general assembly, or general court, of any colony or plantation, in North America, shall have appointed, by act of assembly duly confirmed, a settled salary to the offices of the chief justice and judges of the superior courts, it may be proper that the said chief justice and other judges of the superior courts of such colony shall hold his and their office and offices during their good behavior; and shall not be removed therefrom, but when the said removal shall be adjudged by his Majesty in council, upon a hearing on complaint from the general assembly, or on a complaint from the governor, or council, or the house of representatives, severally, of the colony in which the said chief justice and other judges have exercised the said office."

XIII. "That it may be proper to regulate the courts of admiralty, or vice-admiralty, authorized by the fifteenth chapter of the fourth of George III, in such a manner, as to make the same more commodious to those who sue, or are sued, in the said courts; *and to provide for the more decent maintenance of the judges of the same.*"

SUGGESTIONS FOR STUDY.

I. HOW TO GET A CLEAR UNDERSTANDING OF THE SPEECH.

To the Student:—

You can read Burke's Speech in such a way as to make it the foundation to a full knowledge of the principles of free government and of politics, or you can read it in such a way as to make it a dull and useless grind. To accomplish the former and avoid the latter:

1. Read some good account of the events which led up to the crisis, such as will be found in any of the following:

Fiske, *The American Revolution*, Vol. I, Chapter i.

Channing, *Students' History of the United States*, pp. 131–165.

Channing, *The United States of America*, Cambridge Historical Series, pp. 25–71.

Winsor, *Narrative and Critical History of the United States*, Vol. VI, Chap. i. (*The Conflict Impending.*)

Frothingham, *The Rise of the Republic of the United States.*

Bancroft, *History of the United States*, Vol. III.

Sloane, *The French War and the Revolution*, Chaps. i, ix, x, xi, xii, xiii and xiv. Above all, read the account of the Examination of Franklin before the bar of the House of Commons, Jan. 21, 1766.

If time permits, read a well-written account of the history of England from the accession of the House of Hanover, with particular attention to the career of William Pitt the elder (Earl of Chatham). The writer would particularly recommend the following:

W. E. H. Lecky, *History of England in the Eighteenth Century.*

Sir George Otto Trevelyan, *The Early History of Charles James Fox.*

Sir George Otto Trevelyan, *The American Revolution.*

2. Get a clear idea of the British Government and how it compares in its working methods with that of the United States. Read, above all, Moran's *The English Government.* In studying this remember

first, that the Prime Minister is simply an exalted boss; that his office has exactly the same legal status as that of the boss in an American city or state; that while the *Ministers* of the crown are regularly appointed by the sovereign to offices which have been created by law, the *cabinet* has exactly the same legal status as the informal cabinet of an American boss, i. e., the men whom he calls in for consultation before deciding upon any step; that the Prime Minister, like the boss, holds his position,—not his *legal* position of First Lord of the Treasury, or Secretary of State for Foreign Affairs, or whatever office he may have chosen to accept for himself, but his *political* position of Prime Minister—just as long as the boss holds his political position of boss, i. e., just as long as he can swing the majority of votes and dominate legislation. A very interesting line of thought would be to reason why he and his lieutenants must resign their ministerial offices just as soon as it is evident that they do not control a majority vote in the House of Commons. Understand of course that the king, and the king alone, appoints to office and removes from office, but that the king must act upon the advice of the House of Commons. Further, in order to make it clear to the nation that he (the Prime Minister) has control of the House, it is necessary that every bill which he and his colleagues bring forward must be passed; and that no bill brought forward by the opposition shall ever pass. Gentlemen of the opposition sometimes bring forward bills simply to show to the public at large the plan which they would adopt if they were in office, but when they do bring forward such bills, they understand, as a matter of course, that they cannot pass, and that the mover exposes himself to the ridicule and contempt of the party in control. On the other hand, everything that the ministry proposes is practically certain to go through simply because the ministry proposes it, and has the power to put it through. When a bill brought forward by the opposition does pass, it is taken as *prima facie* evidence that the opposition is in control, and the Prime Minister must either instantly remove the evidence of such hostile control by having the House pass a vote of confidence in the ministry, or must advise the king to dissolve Parliament and call a new election, in the hope that such election will result in a definite majority for him and his party; or he and his colleagues must resign their ministerial positions, and allow those who have gained control of the majority in the House to assume the direction of affairs, advise the king, and fill the offices.

The History of the Reform Bill of 1832, and of several similar measures is interesting as showing where the ministerial majority, clearly foreseeing their certain defeat at the polls if they did not yield to popular demand for given legislation, have first voted down such legislation when it was proposed by the leaders of the opposition, and have then introduced it themselves and passed it, in only very slightly changed form.

II. HISTORICAL OUTLINE

OF THE EVENTS WHICH CAUSED THE AMERICAN REVOLUTION

A. **The Nature of the Colonial Governments and Their Relation to the Crown of England.**

  1. **The Three Kinds of Colonial Government: Charter, Royal, and Proprietary.** Describe each.

  2. **Charters were granted by the King and not by Parliament** —Thwaites, *The Colonies* (*Epochs of American History*).

  3. **The practice of self-government by the Colonies**—Frothingham, *The Rise of the Republic of the United States*, 18–19; Thwaites, *The Colonies*, 54, 61–63; Hart, *Formation of the Union*, 10, 13.

  4. **The Union of the English and Scottish Parliaments in 1707 into the British Parliament**—Green, *Short History*, 714–715. How the people of England came to look upon the new Parliament as having imperial power, while the colonies failed to see that it had any more power over them than either of the two Parliaments which it displaced—Jefferson's *Writings*, I, 6; Green, 758.

  5. **Acquiescence of the Colonies in acts of Parliament which conserved the general interests of the Empire, but jealousy of any encroachment on the right of local self-government**— Winsor's *Narrative and Critical History of the United States*, VI, 5; Goldwin Smith, *The United States*, 29–33; Lecky's *Hist. of England in the XVIIIth Century*, IV, 381; Franklin's *Works*, IV, 208, 218, 262, 284.

6. **The Parsons' Cause.** What was the real significance of the verdict?—Tyler's *Life of Patrick Henry*, 32–49; Wirt's *Patrick Henry*, 31–43; Fiske's *The American Revolution*, I, 21.

B. **The Results of the Seven Years War.**

1. **Debt** (a) of England; (b) of the colonies—Hart, *Formation of the Union*, 37; Larned, *Hist. of the U. S.*, 151; Knight, *Hist. of Eng.*, VI, 257; Fiske, *Amer. Rev.*, I, 15–17; Winsor, *Nar. and Crit.*, VI, 15; Lecky, IV, 51.

2. **Sense of a Lack of Dependence**—Winsor, VI, 14; Adams and Trent, *Hist. of the U. S.*, 89; Lecky, IV, 2–5.

3. **Training as Soldiers**—Trevelyan, *Amer. Rev.*, I, 60–61; Hart, *Formation*, 40; Lecky, IV, 7.

4. **Protection of the New Territory**—Bancroft, III, 33; Hart, *Formation*, 49; Winsor, VI, 16.

5. **The Proclamation Line**—McMaster, *School Hist.*, 110.

C. **The Attitude of England Toward the Colonies.**

1. **General ignorance**—Lecky, IV, 50; Trevelyan, I, 11–18; Elson, *School Hist. of the U. S.*, 221.

2. **"Our subjects in America"**—uttered by a member of Parliament.

3. **Trade and Navigation Laws**—
   a. Their purpose.
   b. The benefits which accrued,—(1) to England
   (2) to the colonies.

   Hart, *Formation*, 44–50; Hart, *American History Told by Contemporaries*, II, 127 (text of the act); Winsor, VI, 2–9; Lecky, IV, 41–48, 52–56; McMaster, *School Hist.*, 108; Elson, 70, 216–218; Coman, *Industrial Hist. of the U. S.*, 76–83; Howard, *Preliminaries of the Revolution*, 47–67; Sloane, *The French War and the Revolution*, 118–120, 124–125; Channing, *U. S.*, 31–33.

D. **Smuggling.**

1. **Reasons for its Prevalence**—Hart, *Formation*, 47; Trevelyan, I, 97–101.

2. **Difficulty of securing a conviction**—Lecky, IV, 47; Elson, 218; Hart, *Contemporaries*, II, 249; Trevelyan, I, 101–102.

3. **Writs of Assistance**—why they were issued—Hart, *Formation*,

47; *Life of Samuel Adams* (American Statesmen Series), chap. iii; Lecky, IV, 48; Winsor, VI, 11 (see footnote); Hart, *Contemporaries*, II, 374 (argument of James Otis against them).

4. **Extension of the powers of the Courts of Admiralty** (read the note on p. 100). Trial without jury—McMaster, *School Hist.*, 112; Hart, *Contemporaries*, II, 396–397.

E. **The Grenville Acts,** 1764–March, 1765—Hart, *Formation*, 44–50; Hart, *Contemporaries*, II, 381; Channing, *U. S.*, 39–48; Winsor, VI, 16, 23–29; Franklin, *Works*, VI, 142–145; Bancroft, III, 59–107; McMaster, 110–114; Lecky, IV, 50–53.

1. **Enforcement of the Navigation Laws**—Trevelyan, I, 97–99; Hart, *Formation*, 17, 19, 44–48; Lecky, IV, 52; Bancroft, III, 34, 35, 59–62; Knight, VI, 271.

2. **Tax on sugar, molasses,** etc.—McMaster, 114; Elson, 218; Winsor, VI, 23, 25; Lecky, IV, 53–54.

3. **The Stamp Tax**—Lecky, IV, 67–79; Bancroft, III, 55, 70–74, 99–104; Hart, *Formation*, 48–53; Fiske, *Amer. Rev.*, I, 15–27; Channing, *U. S.*, 48–56; Larned, *Hist. for Ready Reference, The United States of America, A. D. 1765;* Knight, *Pop. Hist. of Eng.*, VI, 271; Elson, 224; Trevelyan, I, 73–74; Hart, *Contemporaries*, II, 394; Winsor, VI, 15–35 (for text, see MacDonald, *Select Charters*, 281, 305; or *Amer. Hist. Leaflets*, no. 21).

F. **Resistance to the Grenville Acts**—Bancroft, III, chaps. ix and xi.

1. **The Sons of Liberty**—Lecky, IV, 74; Elson, 227; McMaster, *School Hist.*, 116.

2. **The Virginia Resolutions**—Tyler's *Patrick Henry*, chap. v, 61–67; Elson, 230; Lecky, IV, 80; Frothingham, 179–181; MacDonald, *Select Charters*, no. 66; Channing, *U. S.*, Appendix.

3. **The Stamp Act Congress**, October, 1765—Bancroft, III, chap. xii; Winsor, VI, 29; Elson, 227; Fiske, 21; Lecky, IV, 75–79, 89–92.

a. **Declaration of Rights**—Preston, *Documents*, 188–191; MacDonald, *Select Charters*, no. 59; Larned, *Hist. for Ready Reference, U. S., 1765;* Channing, *U. S.*, 108; Elson, 123.

Fiske, I, 93–99; MacDonald, *Select Charters*, 68–71; Bancroft, III, 438, 471–482; Lecky, IV, 165–175.

1. **Boston Port Bill**—Frothingham, 320–326; Mahon, *History of England*, VI, 3; McMaster, *School Hist.*, 120.

2. **Transportation Act**—Trevelyan, I, 76; Lecky, IV, 167.

3. **The Massachusetts Act** (a) The Regulating Act; (b) The Act for the Impartial Administration of Justice—MacDonald, *Select Charters*, nos. 69 and 70; Lecky, IV, 166; Frothingham, 344; Trevelyan, I, 166–176; Fiske, I, 124–126 (resistance).

4. **The Quartering Act**—Lecky, IV, 168.

5. **The Quebec Act**—Lecky, IV, 168.

6. **Proposed Legislation**—"The Starvation Act"—Trevelyan, I, 243–253; MacDonald, *Select Charters*, no. 75.

O. **First Continental Congress**—Lecky, IV, 180; Frothingham, 359; Fiske, I, 100.

1. **Declaration of Rights**—Preston, *Documents*, 192, 199; MacDonald, *Select Charters*, no. 72; Frothingham, 371; John Adams' *Works*, II, 535; Hildreth, *History of the United States*, III, 43; Lecky, IV, 181; Gay, *History of the United States*, III, 341; McMaster, *School Hist.*, 121; Force, *Amer. Archives*, 4th series, I, 915.

2. **Address to the People of the Colonies**—Frothingham, 375.

3. **Address to the Canadians.**

4. **Address to the People of Great Britain**—Lecky, IV, 183; Frothingham, 374.

5. **Petition to the King**—Frothingham, 376–377; MacDonald, *Select Charters*, 77; Force, *Amer. Archives*, 4th series, I, 934; J. Adams' *Works*, I, 159; X, 273.

6. **Non-intercourse Association**—Frothingham, 373–396; Lecky, IV, 182.

III. THE FATE OF THE RESOLUTIONS.

"The first four motions and the last had the previous question put on them; the others were negatived."

THE PREVIOUS QUESTION: This is a mode of procedure to bring the house to action upon the question under consideration. It is so called because it must be determined *previous* to the real question.

As stated by the chairman, it is, "Shall the main question (the one which the house is considering at the time) be now put?" In the British House of Commons the previous question has two uses. The first is to close debate on a pending measure and bring it to immediate vote; the other and more usual is quietly to dispose of a measure on which the house does not wish to commit itself. To illustrate the first use let us suppose a case:—Some resolution proposed by the majority is before the house: the minority are making a desperate effort and are evidently trying to prevent action upon the resolution by prolonging the debate until the majority are tired out and ready to adjourn. At such a juncture the majority may protect itself by moving the previous question. This being moved and seconded, the chairman puts it as above—"*Shall the main question* (the resolution which the house has been debating) be *now* put?" This will naturally receive the votes of the majority and, it being decided in the affirmative, all debate ceases and the resolution is put to vote. This is sometimes called "The Gag Law."

On the other hand, take the case of Burke's first resolution. It was a mere matter of fact. No one could gainsay it. Yet it was an opening wedge, and led to conclusions which the ministry were quite unwilling to admit. They did not wish to vote it down, for that would be denying what everybody knew to be a fact. By moving the previous question themselves, and then voting in the negative, they decide that the main question, i. e., Mr. Burke's resolution, *shall not now be put.* Under the older practice, which obtained in Burke's day, this disposed of it for the session; now it merely suppresses it for that day.

As the *Annual Register* tells us, "The first four motions and the last had the previous question put on them; the others were negatived." If the student will read the sixth and twelfth inclusive he will see that they were measures on which the ministry were very ready to record a decided majority in the negative. We might have expected the fifth to be treated in the same manner as the first four.

Most of the texts on Burke follow the evident misprint which appears in the *Annual Register* and tell us that the previous question was moved and "carried" by 270 to 78. Of course Burke was defeated by such majority, but the previous question was obviously not *carried* but *lost* by that vote.

IV. DEBATE ON MR. BURKE'S RESOLUTIONS FOR CONCILIATION WITH AMERICA.

(From *Parliamentary History*, Vol. XVIII, p. 538.)

The question being put on the first Resolution, Mr. Burke was answered by the Attorney-General, who displayed great dexterity and address in his observations on the plan. The other speakers on that side were, Mr. Jenkinson, Mr. Cornwall, Lord Frederick Campbell, and others. The motions were supported by Lord John Cavendish, Mr. Hotham, Mr. Tuffnell, Mr. Sawbridge, and Mr. Fox, who spoke with the greatest ability and spirit.

The ministerial side did not in general so object to this plan, as repeat and enforce their general arguments on the supremacy of the British Parliament, and in favor of the policy and necessity of American taxation. They denied that the American assemblies ever had, at any time, a legal power of granting a revenue to the crown. That this was the privilege of Parliament only, and could not be communicated to any other body whatsoever: for this

Mr. Jenkinson quoted the famous Act for securing the rights and liberties of the subject, commonly called the Declaration of Right; which, as they insisted, clearly enforced the exclusive right of taxing in Parliament all parts of the King's dominions. The article is as follows, that "Levying money for, or to the use of the crown, by pretense of prerogative, without grant of Parliament, for a longer time, or in other manner than the same is or shall be granted, is illegal." This, he said, was not only prudent but necessary. The right of taxing was inherent in the supreme power; and by being the most essential of all powers, was the most necessary, not only to be reserved in theory, but exercised in practice; or it would, in effect, be lost, and all other powers along with it. It was, he said, a great mistake, that the establishment of a Parliament in Ireland precluded Great Britain from taxing that kingdom. That the right of taxing it had always been maintained, and exercised too, whenever it was thought expedient, and ought undoubtedly always to be so, whenever the British Parliament judged proper; having no other rule in this respect but its own discretion. That all inferior assemblies were only like the corporate towns in England, who had a power, like them, of making by-laws, and nothing more. He recommended the example of the

French government in their provinces called *Pais d'états;* where, though the people seem to grant, yet, in reality, the mode alone of raising the tax is left to the province; the crown always fixing the sum to be raised. These grants are, therefore, not free; but, as one of their own writers, Voltaire, calls them, reputed free; and that the people were so well satisfied with this reputed freedom, that they never have refused to grant, except once, when the states of Languedoc were refractory: but an army being sent to reduce them, they were brought to obedience, and have been ever since perfectly quiet. This was the substance of Mr. Jenkinson's speech.

Lord Frederick Campbell took up the same maxims, and maintained them with great warmth; declaring, that he thought any minister ought to be impeached, who suffered the grant of any sort of revenue from the colonies to the crown. Indeed it was possible, that such a practice in time of war, from the necessity of the case, might be tolerated, but that a revenue in time of peace could not be granted by the assemblies, without subverting the constitution.

Mr. Jenkinson moved the previous question, upon the first Resolution. Upon this the House divided. The Noes went forth.

Tellers.

Yeas { Mr. Hotham . . . . } 78
     { Mr. Byng . . . . }

Noes { Lord Cranbone . . . . . . } 270
     { Mr. Cooper . . . . }

So it passed in the negative. The second, third, fourth and thirteenth Resolutions had also the previous question put on them. The others were negatived.

During this debate the standing order for the exclusion of strangers was strictly enforced.

"On this motion, and on the whole matter, the debate was long and animated. It was objected, in general, that these resolutions abandoned the whole object for which we were contending. That in words indeed they did not give up the right of taxing; but they did so in effect. The first resolution, they said, was artfully worded, as containing in appearance nothing but matters of fact; but if adopted, consequences would follow highly prejudicial to the public good. That the mere truth of a proposition did not of course make it necessary or proper to resolve it. As they had frequently resolved not to admit the unconstitutional claims of the Americans, they could not admit resolutions directly leading to them. They had no assurance that if they should adopt these propositions the Americans would make any dutiful returns on their side; and thus the scheme, pursued through so many difficulties, of compelling that refractory people to contribute their fair proportion to the expenses of the whole empire, would fall to the ground. The House of Lords would not, they said, permit another plan somewhat of the same kind so much as to lie on their table; and the House of Commons had in this session already adopted one, which they judged to be conciliatory upon a ground more consistent with the supremacy of Parliament. It was asserted, that the American assemblies had made provision upon former occasions; but this, they said, was only then pressed by their own immediate danger; and for their own local use. But if the dispositions of the colonies had been as favorable as they were represented, still it was denied, that the American assemblies ever had a legal power of granting a revenue to the crown. This they insisted to be the privilege of Parliament only; and a privilege which could not be communicated to any other body whatsoever. In support of this doctrine, they quoted the following clause from that palladium of the English constitution, and of the rights and liberties of the subject, commonly called the Bill, or Declaration of Rights; viz. that 'Levying money for, or to the use of the crown, by pretense of prerogative, without grant of Parliament, for a longer time, or in other manner, than the same is or shall be granted, is illegal.'

"This clause, they insisted, clearly enforced the exclusive right in Parliament of taxing every part of the empire. And this right, they said, was not only prudent, but necessary. The right of taxation must be inherent in the supreme power; and being the most essential of all others, was the most necessary, not only to be reserved in theory, but exercised in practice; or it would, in effect, be lost, and all other powers along with it. This principle was carried so far, that it was said any minister ought to be impeached, who suffered the grant of any sort of revenue from the colonies to the crown. That such a practice in time of war, might possibly be tolerated from the necessity of the case; but that a revenue in time of peace could not be granted by any of the assemblies, without subverting the constitution. In the warmth of prosecuting this idea, it was asserted, by more than one gentleman on that side, that the establishment of a Parliament in Ireland, did not by any means preclude Great Britain from taxing that kingdom whenever it was thought necessary. That that right had always been maintained, and exercised too, whenever it was judged expedient; and that the British Parliament had no other rule in that exercise, than its own discretion. That all inferior assemblies in this empire, were only like the corporate towns in England, which had a power, like them, of making by-laws, for their own municipal government, and nothing more.

"On the other side, it was urged, that the clause in the Declaration of Rights, so much relied on, was calculated merely to restrain the prerogative, from the raising of any money within the realm, without the consent of Parliament; but that it did not at all reach, nor was intended to interfere, with the taxes levied, or grants passed by legal assemblies out of the kingdom, for the public service. On the contrary, Parliament knew at the time of passing that law, that the Irish grants were subsisting, and taxes constantly levied in consequence of them, without their once thinking, either then or at any other time, of censuring the practice, or condemning the mode as unconstitutional. It was also said, that different parliaments at different periods, had not only recognized the right, but gratefully acknowledged the benefit which the public derived from the taxes levied, and the grants passed by the American assemblies. As to the distinction taken of a time of war and the necessity of the case; they said it was frivolous and wholly groundless. The power of the subject in granting, or of the crown in receiving, no way differs in time of war, from the same powers in time of peace; nor is any distinction on such a supposition made in the article of the Bill of Rights. They argued, therefore, that this article of the Bill of Rights is confined to what it was always thought confined, the prerogative in this kingdom; and bound indeed the crown; but could not, in securing the rights and liberties of the subject in this kingdom, intend to annihilate them everywhere else. That as the constitution had permitted the Irish Parliament and the American assemblies to make grants to the crown; and that experience had shown, that these grants had produced both satisfaction and revenue, it was absurd to risk all in favor of theories of supremacy, unity, sovereign rights, and other names, which hitherto had led to nothing but confusion and beggary on all sides, and would continue to produce the same miserable effects, as long as they were persisted in. That the mover had very wisely avoided these speculative questions, and confined himself to experience; and it would be well if they could persuade themselves to follow that example. The previous question was moved on the first proposition, and carried [1] by 270 to 78." (*Annual Register.*)

V. THE REASON FOR EXTENDING THE JURISDICTION OF THE COURTS OF ADMIRALTY.

So nearly universal was smuggling in the colonies at this time that it was practically impossible to secure a jury that did not have some one who was either himself a smuggler or was closely associated with some one else who was. Finding it impossible to secure a conviction in a civil court, the British ministry had the alternative of either giving up all attempts to enforce the revenue laws or else of providing a court that would convict. The discipline of the British navy was maintained by naval courts-martial or Courts of Admiralty, and the ministry decided that if the officers who constituted these courts were given a share in the proceeds of the condemned vessels, the cases brought before them would probably result in a reasonably large percentage of convictions.

Courts of Admiralty like other military courts, consisted of: 1. A board of officers who acted as jury; 2. A judge advocate who combined in himself the offices of judge, attorney for the prosecution, and attorney for the defendant. In theory, this judge advocate was simply to ask questions, and thereby bring out the truth. This form of court, unknown to Anglo-Saxon institutions, was borrowed from the military practice of Continental Europe. The Court of High Commission, and the Star Chamber were organized on this principle, and were, therefore, odious to Englishmen. So long as the judge advocate was the personification of justice, the court might do efficient work, but when his fees consisted in a share of the money received from the sale of vessels condemned in his own court, he might very possibly be

---

[1] See extract from *Parliamentary History*, page 97.

suspected of prejudice. Since practically all trading vessels of the colonies were engaged in smuggling, it was hardly worth while for the owner of a vessel caught in the act to proceed to Halifax with his witnesses, etc., and there plead his cause before such a court. (Compare the expression "Gone to Halifax.") He usually let the matter go by default, and built another ship.

VI. PROTEST AGAINST PASSING THE BILL FOR RE-STRAINING THE TRADE AND COMMERCE OF THE NEW ENGLAND COLONIES.

It has been maintained by some that this protest, which the Whig lords filed against the passage of "The Starvation Act," was written, not by the men who signed it, but by Burke, for the reason that Lord Rockingham was their leader, and Burke was closely associated with him. Study it and determine from its style whether there is sufficient similarity to give good ground for such a supposition. Note the use of words, the turn of phrases, the structure of sentences, and above all the principles upon which it is based.

In the *Parliamentary History*, Vol. XVIII, pp. 292, 294, 1351, will be found other similar protests. If you have access to that work, read those protests also and compare the style with the Speech on Conciliation with America, and decide whether they sound as if they were written by Burke.

The following Protest was entered:
"Dissentient,
1st, "Because the attempt to coerce by famine, the whole body of the inhabitants of great and populous provinces, is without example in the history of this, or perhaps of any civilized nation; and is one of those unhappy inventions, to which Parliament is driven by the difficulties which daily multiply upon us, from an obstinate adherence to an unwise plan of government. We do not know exactly the extent of the combination against our commerce in New England, and the other colonies; but we do know the extent of the punishment we inflict upon it, which is universal, and includes all the inhabitants: amongst these, many are admitted to be innocent; and several are alleged by ministers to be, in their sense, even meri-

torious. That government which attempts to preserve its authority by destroying the trade of its subjects, and by involving the innocent and guilty in a common ruin, if it acts from a choice of such means, confesses itself unworthy; if from inability to find any other, admits itself wholly incompetent to the ends of its institution.

2dly, "Because the English merchants are punished without guilt, real or pretended, on their part. The people of the proscribed provinces, though failing in their duty to government, ought to be permitted to discharge their obligations to commerce. Without their fishery this is impossible. The merchants of England entertain no fears for their debts, except from the steps which are said to be taken in their favor. Eight hundred thousand pounds of English property, belonging to London alone, is not to be trifled with, or sacrificed to the projects of those who have constantly failed in every expectation which they have held out to the public, and who are become more bigoted to methods of violence, in proportion to the experience of their inefficacy, and the mischievous consequences which attend them.

3dly, "Because the people of New England, besides the natural claim of mankind to the gifts of Providence on their own coast, are specially entitled to the fishery by their charters, which have never been declared forfeited. These charters, we think, (notwithstanding the contempt with which the idea of public faith has been treated), to be of material consideration. The Bill therefore not growing out of any judicial process, seems equally a violation of all natural and all civil right.

4thly, "Because we conceive that the attempt which has been made to bribe the nation into an acquiescence in this arbitrary Act, by holding out to them, (by evidence at the bar), the spoils of the New England fishery, worth upwards of £3,000,000 a year, to be a scheme full of weakness and indecency; of indecency, because it may be suspected that the desire of the confiscation has created the guilt; weak, because it supposes that whatever is taken from the colonies, is of course to be transferred to ourselves. We may trample on the rules of justice; but we cannot alter the nature of things. We cannot convey to Great Britain the advantages of situation which New England possesses for the fishery. If the value of the commodity should be enhanced at the foreign market by the exclusion of so large a part of the supply, it may either greatly injure the sale of the commodity itself, or put the consumers on new articles of consumption, or new methods of supply, to the just ruin of those who, deluded by avarice, have chosen, from the vain hope of an enhanced market, to disturb the natural, settled, and beneficial course of traffic.

5thly, "Because we do not apprehend that the topic so much insisted upon by a lord high in office, in favor of this project, namely, the cowardice of his Majesty's American subjects, to have any weight in itself, or to be at all agreeable to the dignity of sentiment which ought to characterize this House. We do not think it true, that any part of the subjects of this empire are defective in bravery. It is to the last degree improper to act upon such a supposition; as it must highly disgrace our arms in case of misfortune, and must take away all honor from them in case of success. Nothing can tend more effectually to defeat the purposes of all our coercive measures, than to let the people against whom they are intended know, that we think our authority founded in their baseness; that their resistance will give them some credit, even in our own eyes; and that we attribute their obedience only to their want of courage. This is to call for resistance, and to provoke rebellion by the most powerful of all motives, which can act upon men of any degree of spirit and sensibility.

6thly, "Because the interdict from fishing and commerce, is not to be terminated by any certain and definite act to be done by the party interdicted, but its duration depends solely on the will of the governors and majority of the council in some of the provinces; upon their mere arbitrary opinion of the state of commerce. In two of the proscribed provinces, the interdict is made to depend on the same arbitrary will in much worse hands, those of mere custom-house officers. A power of such magnitude is not fit to be delegated to any man, however wise or however exalted.

"But to deliver over several hundred thousands of our fellow creatures to be starved at the mere pleasure of persons in certain subordinate situations, and some of them in an office always more or less suspicious and obnoxious, and necessary to be watched and guarded, rather than vested with absolute power over all; and this without any rule to guide their discretion, without any penalty to deter from an abuse of it; is a strain of such tyranny, oppression, and absurdity, as we believe never was deliberately entertained by any grave assembly.

Lastly, "Because the Bill, though in appearance a measure of retaliation only, upon a supposition that the colonies have been the first aggressors by their association not to import goods from Great Britain, yet is in truth a most cruel enforcement of former oppressions; and that association is no more than a natural consequence of antecedent and repeated injuries. And since the restraint of this Bill is not to be taken off till the several colonies shall agree to receive again all goods whatsoever from Great Britain, and to pay all the duties imposed by Parliament, not excepting those upon tea; and since three of them must apply through the medium of the new council of Massachusetts Bay, and the last mentioned province is obliged not only to acknowledge the new charter, but submit in all respects to the severe conditions of the Port Bill, before they can be released from their hardships; since these are the terms, upon which this proscription is to cease, and the colonies must therefore submit to be the slaves instead of the subjects of Great Britain; this Bill in its principle is both arbitrary and unjust. And as we do not conceive any ground of expectation that the provinces will yield to such hard conditions, a civil war, which may probably end in the total separation of the colonies from the mother country, will too naturally be the consequence of this Bill; in respect of which, as well as for the other reasons hereby assigned, we do most solemnly and heartily protest against the same.

(Signed)—ABINGDON, CRAVEN, ABERGAVENNY, STANHOPE, LEINSTER, WYCOMBE, RICHMOND, DEVONSHIRE, TORRINGTON, ROCKINGHAM, CAMDEN, EFFINGHAM, PONSONBY, CHOLMONDELEY, FITZWILLIAM, MANCHESTER."

NOTES.

(Numerals in heavy type refer to the pages of the text, the lighter ones to the lines.)

17: 1. Chair. To whom alone must any speaker in any deliberative Assembly address his remarks? What superstition is it that Burke is apologizing for in the beginning of his speech?

17: 7. The grand penal bill. Read note 2 on p. 17 and tell why this bill was called " The Starvation Act." The bill was amended in the House of Lords so as to make it apply to all the colonies.

19: 11. Which I dare not name. Why dare not Burke name the situation in the colonies?

Remember that in 1766, the year when the Stamp Act was repealed, Lord Rockingham, a Whig, was Prime Minister, and that Burke and this Mr. Fuller (l. 15) were both members of his party. What party is referred to in the words " our conduct " (l. 22), " their authors " (l. 24), " charging us " (l. 25), " whilst we accused " (l. 26)?

19: 29. Play the game out. What is it to " play the game out "? When Burke made his speech which side was having its " innings," and which side was " out "? What is the reason for all this about the conversation with Mr. Rose Fuller?

20: 13–14. Ridicule, disgrace. What is the " ridicule " and the " disgrace " to which he refers?

21: 2. Influence . . . adventitious. What gentleman on the government benches opposite to Burke possessed adventitious influence?

21: 7. The proposition is peace. Just what has Burke accomplished up to this point? Give the reason why he utters each one of the first eight paragraphs. The six paragraphs covering pages 21, 22 and 23 constitute the STATUS. Tell what each paragraph accomplishes by itself, and what is accomplished as a whole by the six.

21: 17. Former unsuspecting confidence of the colonies in the mother country. This is put in italics because Burke borrowed it from John Dickinson, the " Pennsylvania Farmer." His *Letters of* *a Farmer* are difficult of access, but they are very well worth reading if you want to know how the Americans felt at this time. Turn to page 76 of this text and read Burke's refutation (page 76, l. 11 to page 80, l. 2) of Lord North's plan before you go further. After reading this refutation do you think that Lord North sincerely wished to conciliate the colonies by his project?

21: 22. My idea is nothing more. Read this paragraph aloud several times just to see what Burke has done in the sound of words and the form of his sentences.

21: 32. Project. Why does Burke call it a *project* instead of a *resolution?*

23: 6-8. Great . . . itself. Explain fully, and illustrate from something which you have seen in daily life, the truth of Burke's statement.

23: 15. The capital leading questions, etc. What part of the speech does this introduce? Into what two parts does it divide the rest of the speech?

23: 30-33. I shall therefore endeavor, etc. Here begins the third division of the speech, THE STATEMENT OF FACTS, and first he takes up material facts.

23: 34. The first thing, etc. Do you believe that Burke is fair and conservative in his statement regarding population? What means has he used to create this impression in your mind?

24: 6. But whether I put, etc. How does he forestall the effect of any attempt at refutation of his figures?

24: 17. I put this consideration, etc. The following from Dr. Johnson's *Taxation no Tyranny* shows you what the king's friends thought about the situation. Remember that Dr. Johnson was one of the leaders of English thought in his day. Do you conclude after reading this that the American Revolution could have been prevented?

" But while we are melting in silent sorrow, and in the transports of delicious pity, dropping both the sword and balance from our hands, another friend of the *Americans* thinks it better to awaken another passion, and tries to alarm our interest, or excite our veneration, by accounts of their greatness and their opulence, of the fertility of their land, and the splendor of their Towns. We then begin to consider the question with more evenness of mind, are ready to conclude that those restrictions are not very oppressive which have been found consistent with this speedy growth of prosperity, and begin to think it reasonable, that they who thus flourish under the protection of our Government, should contribute something towards its expense.

"But we are then told that the Americans, however wealthy, cannot be taxed; that they are the descendants of men who left all for liberty, and that they have constantly preserved the principles and stubbornness of their progenitors; that they are too obstinate for persuasion, and too powerful for constraint; that they will laugh at argument, and defeat violence; that the Continent of *North America* contains three millions, not of men merely, but of Whigs; of Whigs fierce for liberty, and disdainful of dominion; that they multiply with the fecundity of their own rattlesnakes, so that every quarter of a century doubles their numbers.

"Men accustomed to think themselves masters, do not love to be threatened. This talk is, I hope, commonly thrown away, or raises passions different from those which it intended to excite. Instead of terrifying the *English* hearer to tame acquiescence, it disposes him to hasten the experiment of bending obstinacy before it is become yet more obdurate, and convinces him that it is necessary to attack a Nation thus prolific, while we may yet hope to prevail. When he is told through what extent of territory we must travel to subdue them, he recollects how far, a few years ago, we traveled in their defense. When it is urged that they will shoot up like the hydra, he naturally considers how the hydra was destroyed."

25: 19. I have in my hand two accounts. Sum up in brief what Burke says about commerce. Why does he say it? What bearing has it on the speech?

Entire Trade of England	. . . .	1704 ———
Entire Trade of England	. . . .	1772 ———
Colonial Trade	. . . .	1704 ———
Colonial Trade	. . . .	1772 ———

What means does Burke use to make his hearers believe the truth of his statement? What rule can you formulate from this as to how a debater should handle statistics?

27: 12. All reasoning concerning our mode of treating them. How again does Burke forestall the arguments of his opponents on the fact of the growth of colonial commerce?

27: 15. Mr. Speaker, etc. This paragraph is typical of one element in Burke's style. Some critics maintain that so beautiful a paragraph as this interferes with the purpose of the oration. Read it carefully and tell what you think about it.

28: 26. Excuse me, Sir, etc. Another lesson to a debater on how to use statistics. What does Burke gain by this paragraph? Remember once more what he is trying to do with these statistics.

29: 16. Their agriculture. Why does Burke say all this about the agriculture of the colonies?

29: 29. Their fisheries. When Lord North's " Starvation Act " was introduced, some members in the House inquired whether, if the colonists were forbidden to fish on the banks of Newfoundland there might not result a shortage in the supply of fish for the British markets. The following from a petition of English fish merchants explains Burke's use of the words " for they seemed even to excite your envy " (l. 30).

BILL TO RESTRAIN THE TRADE.

A Petition of the Merchants, Traders, and principal Inhabitants of the Town and County of *Poole*, was also presented to the House and read, setting forth—

That the Petitioners observe that a Petition is presented to the House from the Lord Mayor, Aldermen, and Commons of the City of *London*, in Common Council assembled, against the Bill mentioned in the preceding Petition; and that the Petitioners beg leave to observe, that the restraints intended to be laid upon the *Newfoundland* Fishery of the Colonies, mentioned in the said Bill, if carried into a Law, will not by any means be injurious to Commerce, as the Petitioners against the Bill conceive, because the foreign markets can be amply supplied by extending the *Newfoundland* Fishery, of the subjects resident in England; and that the annual produce of the *Newfoundland* Fishery, carried on by subjects resident in the mother country, exceeds five hundred thousand Pounds; and that the *Newfoundland* Fishery of the mother country is a constant nursery of Seamen for the Navy, that great bulwark of the Nation, every fifth man employed being, by the tenth of *William* the Third, obliged to be a Landman, a consideration of infinite weight, the Petitioners imagine, and this the more especially, as the profits of the trade center entirely in this kingdom; and that the profits of the *Newfoundland* Fishery carried on by the Colonies mentioned in this bill, do not center here; nor is the *Newfoundland* Fishery of the Colonies a nursery of Seamen for the Fleet, because the *Americans* are not obliged by law to make use of the Landmen, nor are the *American* Seamen compellable like the *British* Seamen, to serve their country in times of war; the

Petitioners are therefore greatly alarmed, lest a Petition from so respectable a body as the Lord Mayor, Aldermen, and Commons of *London*, should operate not only to their prejudice, but to the general prejudice of the Kingdom, on a point of such importance to the national prosperity, humbly submit the foregoing facts to the consideration of the House, and soliciting, no less for their own immediate advantage, than for the universal benefit of their country, such encouragement of the *British* Fishery to *Newfoundland*, as the Parliament shall think proper.

31 : 16. First, Sir, etc. Burke here interrupts his *Statement of Facts* to introduce a negative argument. Why is it best that this be brought in here, rather than in his general *Refutation of Objections?* After reading this *Digression* what do you think of Burke as a prophet?

32 : 6. Pursued to a fault. Explain.

32 : 10–13. These, Sir . . . a third consideration? What is the first and the second? Here he resumes his *Statement of Facts.*

32 : 22. Shuffle from them by chicane. How did England attempt to " shuffle from them by chicane " their right to tax themselves? Explain carefully in detail. It is worth while to read in Burke's Speech on American Taxation what he says about " A Preambulary Tax."

When did the New England colonists emigrate?

Why did they emigrate from England?

What great struggle was then going on?

32 : 24. This fierce spirit of liberty. What has the cause of this spirit of liberty to do with his argument?

32 : 36. Abstract liberty, etc. Explain carefully this line and apply your explanation to mathematical and other abstract qualities.

34 : 20. Dissenting churches. What are the " dissenting churches " in England?

34 : 34. A refinement on the principle of resistance. How is this true of the Congregational form of church government? How are the Baptist and Quaker churches governed? What is an established church?

35 : 4. Legal rights. What does Burke assume the " legal rights " of the Church of England to have been in Massachusetts? Find out what you can about Archbishop Laud. What had he to do with hastening the emigration to America?

35 : 8. Stream of foreigners. What nations contributed to that " stream of foreigners "?

36: 11. And most do read. What is the significance of this ex-planatory statement? What inference regarding the state of educa-tion of England as compared with America at that time? Read in some history of the Revolution how the colonists continued to hold town meetings in Boston after August 1, 1774, without permission of the authorities, and contrary to the Massachusetts Act.

36: 27. Honorable and learned friend. The attorney-general, Mr. Thurlow, as well as his associate, the solicitor-general, Mr. Wed-derburn, had been on both sides politically, and doubtless appreciated Burke's remark.

38: 5. The whole of the force . . . all his borders. Explain care-fully and illustrate.

How does Burke try here to make it easy for Parliament to concede to America?

38: 21. I do not mean to commend, etc. At this point Burke has completed what part of his speech, and what part does he here begin?

39: 25. They have formed a government. Read carefully in Ban-croft or Frothingham an account of how Massachusetts maintained peace and order without any government that had been sanctioned by England.

40: 15. Anarchy is found tolerable. Remember that there was no "anarchy" in the colonies. It was simply a complete absence of government authorized by Parliament, but the effective presence of the government organized amongst the people by the committees of correspondence.

40: 15. A vast province has now subsisted, etc. Read in Bancroft, Vol. IV, pages 43–54.

40: 20. Our late experience has taught us, that many of those fun-damental principles, etc. State in the form of a principle one or more of those principles. State in like form one or more of those "other far more important and far more powerful principles, *which entirely over-rule those we had considered as omnipotent*" (ll. 24–25). Remember that in stating a principle you will not use a proper noun, for it must apply to all cases.

40: 25. I am much against any further experiments. What does this sentence tell you of Burke's political ideas? Was he a Progressive or a Conservative?

41: 6. But, Sir. What has Burke accomplished in the three paragraphs preceding this? What does he accomplish in this paragraph? Why does he take up the three courses in this order?

41: 29. As the growing population. What does the fact of this "applause" (l. 31) indicate regarding the feeling of many Englishmen toward America at this time? Under the circumstances do you think the American Revolution could have been prevented?

42: 2. Avarice of desolation. What figure of speech?

42: 19. Hordes of English Tartars. How did the Battle of King's Mountain prove Burke a prophet here?

43: 18. But when I consider that we have colonies for no purpose but to be serviceable to us. This may sound like sarcasm, but it isn't.

44: 1. Your speech would betray you. It is worth while to study how Burke and Webster and other great English-speaking orators gained their power in the use of words. It was chiefly by having committed to memory a large part of the English Bible. Burke also knew by heart many other English authors, particularly, Milton.

45: 12. The ocean remains. You cannot pump this dry. This is called *reductio ad absurdum* or bringing an argument down to an absurdity. Can you see why he put this matter of distance last?

45: 26. At this proposition I must pause a moment. This paragraph is typical of Burke's habit of thought and expression.

46: 28. The claim of a privilege seems, etc. Illustrate this by a real or supposed incident taken from school life. Note that it says: " a *claim* of a privilege " and not the act of asking for a privilege.

50: 29. To admit the people of our colonies into an interest in the constitution. In what way does Burke propose to do this? Refer at once to his resolutions and read them carefully, and note that he does NOT propose to grant representation in Parliament.

53: 12. But the colonies will go further. This of course is what Burke's opponents say.

55: 6. Your standard could never be advanced an inch before your privileges. Explain this carefully.

55: 16. You changed the people. Read in some English history how England " changed the people " and " altered the religion " of Ireland. When was the Church of England disestablished in Ireland?

56: 4. By the lucrative amount. This is irony.

56: 6. Your Irish pensioners. What does Burke imply by this sentence? Look up carefully the word " pensioners."

57: 26. The tyranny of a free people. Explain carefully what " free people " is meant.

59: 23. What did Parliament. What treatment by Parliament of certain petitions, addresses, etc., does Burke have in mind here?

60: 26. But America is virtually represented. This of course was the contention of Burke's opponents. What is meant by a " virtual representation "? Is the representation of the women in your community in the government virtual, or actual and palpable? Study this paragraph as a good example of cumulative argument.

62: 7. My resolutions, therefore. Commit to memory this paragraph. It is the keynote to the whole speech.

62: 8. Taxation of America by grant. What is the difference between taxation by " grant," and taxation by " imposition "? Are the taxes which support your school raised by grant or imposition? Are the taxes levied in the city of Washington levied by grant or imposition?

63: 24. I did not dare. Again, was Burke a Progressive or a Conservative?

66: 3. What habitual offenders. This is irony. Read page 98.

74: 18. All government, . . . is founded on compromise and barter. Is this true? Give instances tending to prove the truth or falsity of the statement.

75: 24. It is said. Burke implies that the unity of the Empire would not be dissolved by conceding to the Americans the right to grant their own taxes, because that unity was preserved entire when the same right was granted to Wales, Chester and Durham. There is a fallacy in his argument here. Find it.

80: 27. Experience is a cheat. Is it true that people pay taxes only when *not* compelled to? Prove or disprove this statement of Burke's. Did the people who paid in taxes the money to build your schoolhouse enjoy " the power of refusal " (l. 26)? Do the people who pay the taxes for the support of the American Navy enjoy this same power? How does the United States government get six hundred million dollars a year to spend?

82: 30. For that service. It is well to commit the following five paragraphs to memory. Why are Canada and Australia still under the British flag? Is it because they don't dare secede? If Burke were an American to-day where would he stand politically?

(1). no representation

(2) taxation a burden

(3). distance

(4). competent assemblies

(5) grants acknowledged

(6). more acceptible to colonist – amirable to crown

f. Three subsidiaries proposition

    1. Repeal penal laws

    2. Secure fair judicature

    3. Regulate ports of

Conclusion

I. Conciliation on the basis of these resolutions would affect neither authority.

    1. grievance would not extend to other legislations

        (1) colonists have not gone beyond the question of taxation

        (2) america has no interest contrary to the glory of England

    2. Power to make grants would not destroy the unity of the empire

        (1). Ireland has a separate gov.

II. Objections to Lord North's plan.

    a. Burke's plan will be more satisfactory than L. N.

        1. Ransom by auction is an experiment

        2. To tax the colonies in the cabinet is unconstitutional

        3. It does not meet the complaints of the colonies

        4. It will plunge Eng. into inextricable difficulties

        5. It will yield a smaller revenue or a permanent quarrel

        6. Impossible to provide for punctual payments

b. to prosecute spirit of criminals
    1. cannot indict a whole people.
    2. plead for privilege without rebelling
    3. England Cannot judge in her own case.
    4. criminal punishment has not proved expedient.

c. comply with spirit as necessary.

III. What should the concession be?

a. Concession should conciliate.

b. Right to tax is irrelevant (is not question).
    1. question of policy.
    2. essential to secure peace.
    3. there is no argument that the repeal of
    tax laws would repeal trade laws
        (1) trade laws useless.
        (2). Revenue laws produce no revenue.
        (3) Revenue laws do not protect Trade laws.

c. It is not fair to assume that concession as to revenue would lead to a demand of greater concessions.

d. concession is a accordance with the genius of E. Constitution
    1. It has been successful in four cases.
    2. These ex. apply to Amer.

e. America should be allowed to pay by grants.
    1. Impossible to give colonies representation
    2. Stopping Taxation will bring tranquillity
    3. Six resolutions to secure peace of colonies